# ADVAITA VEDANTA
## QUESTION OF THE REAL

## Inclusive of KUNDALINI YOGA
### Rising to the Thousand-petalled Lotus

ORDO ASTRI

# ADVAITA VEDANTA

## QUESTION OF

# THE REAL

### INCLUSIVE OF KUNDALINI YOGA

OLIVER ST. JOHN

*Advaita Vedanta—Question of The Real*
Inclusive of *Kundalini Yoga—Rising to the Thousand-petalled Lotus*
© Oliver St. John 2025

Cover design © Oliver St. John 2025
ISBN 978-1-7391549-7-4
Ordo Astri Imprimatur
www.ordoastri.org

*It* is the smallest and the greatest and yet it is truly neither small nor great for *It* does not occupy space and time; Atma is without birth and death and has no cause other than what *It* is, always has been and always will be. Atma is eternal, infinite, immutable and untransmissible.

Atma (Self) and Brahma (Universal) are One and not two things.

# CONTENTS

# Preface

*Sophia is our Guiding Light.*

The Advaitan Way of Self-Realisation involves a prolonged and deep enquiry into the nature of the Self. By the Self, we do not mean the ego or the psychic domain of the person, but the true Self called Atma. We must make it clear that this *viveka* 'enquiry' has nothing to do with any kind of 'self-exploration' in the ordinary way that is meant. We use the term 'Self-Realisation' even though it has, in the words of one scholar, become a cliché—we will go further and say that the term has suffered abuse. What better thing to do than to restore it to its true meaning? Sanskrit words do not have a direct translation in any modern language that can be put in one or two words. We have to use special terms created from our own language to approximate the meaning. 'Self-Realisation' is a short way of saying 'direct knowledge of the supreme principial reality, gained not by inference or belief'. To the religious person or *bhakti* devotee, this is knowledge of God, in whatever name or form God is worshipped. Advaita goes one step even beyond that and claims it is possible to know the Supreme Identity, otherwise called Brahma Nirguna, 'Brahma with no attributes', that is to say, beyond name and form. This is no small claim; however, seers and sages for millennia have asserted its truth.

The Gnostics, a noun that is formed from the Greek *gnosis*, phonetically similar and identical in meaning to the Sanskrit *jnana*, 'non-ordinary knowledge', risked being done to death in horrible ways if they disclosed this truth. For that reason the Gnosis, or what is called Brahma-jnana in the Sanskrit, all but died out completely in the Western world, which is still largely ignorant of Advaita Vedanta, though study of the subject has increased through the efforts of certain monastic lineages, and the fact that many new translations of the core texts have been produced, some of these of a much higher quality than were previously available. Nonetheless, if we turn to a dictionary to look up Gnosticism we will find there that it is supposed by the experts that write these things to be something to do with 'mysticism', which it certainly is not! Mysticism must be attached to a religion, and involves emotional experience. Gnosis requires no religious attachment and rests on exact science, though of course that science is of an ancient and traditional kind, no longer understood by Western pundits let alone the man in the street.

i

In this book, we make no attempt to comment on or expound on the source texts of Advaita directly, which in some ways would be rather pretentious in any case given the Hindu commentaries that exist on the three major works of Advaita: The *Brahma Sutras with Bhashya* of Shankaracharya, the *Bhagavad Gita* with Shankara's commentary, and the *Upanishads* with commentary from the same. The commentaries of Sri Shankaracharya on these works have by now been translated into English and some of these are good—we are happy to recommend books to the interested student. Our basis for the subject matter of the present work is in the main part based upon four smaller works of Shankaracharya and other Advaitan sages, which we shall name here:

*Drg Drsya Viveka* (attributed to Bhārati Tirtha).
*Aparokshanubhuti of Sri Shankaracharya.*
*Siddhāntabindu of Srimat Madhusūdana Sarasvat.*
*Dakshinamurti Stotra with Manasollasa* (Sri Shankaracharya).

One should not expect that the above-mentioned books would be anything like this present work. They give the text in Sanskrit letters, a very concise commentary and then some notes and references. We should also mention our own works on the Patañjali Yoga, in theory and practice, which is needed as a support to the practice of Advaita:

*Thunder Perfect Gnosis—Intellectual Flower of Mind.*
*Metamorphosis—Hermetic Science and Yoga Power.*

In the latter work, we began to introduce Advaitan Self-Realisation, as that, in spite of its apparent simplicity is very advanced. Advaita can be practiced alongside of Patañjali Yoga but there is a point of departure, where Advaita then goes one or two steps further. Also, the yoga path as according to the commentaries on the *Yoga-Sutras*, culminates in a goal called *kaivalya*. While *kaivalya* can be regarded in some ways as no different than *moksha* liberation or 'deliverance', the word implies that one becomes a self-isolated 'star' or monad—an idea that was taken up by some modern occultists as well as the philosopher Leibniz, from whom they learned it. This is the reason why pundits and even some modern day Advaitan masters have said that yoga is 'dualistic'. We differ from that view as it rests on how things are theoretically understood and written about and not on practical experience; but as one interpretation at least of *kaivalya* is indisputably 'isolation', we reject it absolutely. It is better to follow yoga up to the point of knowledge of the pure I-sense and thereafter to adopt the Advaitan Raja Yoga of the *avatara* Shankaracharya.

That is, in any case, how we practice and teach it, and it is implicit in this present work, which is nonetheless not only aimed at advanced practitioners but is also aimed at the novice or beginner, and even the interested outsider. Why do we use the term 'outsider'? All traditions agree that neither yoga nor initiation can be worked from out of a book, without a guru. Books and the learning they provide are an indispensible support but the word must be heard from a valid teacher—that is a guru in fact, one that has direct knowledge of that which he is teaching.

In view of the above, it may seem something of a contradiction to have included with this small volume an illustrated outline of the lotuses, chakras and *bija mantras* of Kundalini Yoga. The practice of this is most decidedly not for beginners, only advanced practitioners that have a qualified guru to instruct them. As we have pointed out in the introduction to that concise work, the chakra schema has been much maligned and misused and we can at least attempt to put the record straight here. The further question is what can it have to do with Advaita Vedanta? Advaitans do not usually condemn such practices while they may certainly express strong reservations about them. Advaita regards all the practices of yoga as a useful and in most cases very necessary support to the realisation of the Self or Supreme Identity called Brahma or *sat-chit-anan*da, pure being, consciousness and bliss. Kundalini Yoga can be studied theoretically, and with great profit to those who are serious spiritual seekers. It agrees with the whole subject of the Vedas, even though some have regarded it as a somewhat wayward science. Furthermore, those who are qualified to practice it with a guru will find here all the essential principles, and without any of the by now common distortions that come about through metaphysical incomprehension.

*Sophia be-with-us forever.*

Oliver St. John

West Penwith Peninsula Cornwall Sol in ♒ Luna in ♊ 2025

# Nihilism and the Western Malaise

Nihilism, viewed one way, is an affliction of will, although Sri Shankaracharya put it less delicately as a matter of simple ignorance. It may seem strange to begin a book that serves as an introduction to Advaita Vedanta Non-dualism, which is primarily a Hindu *darshana*, with a critique, albeit a brief one, of the corrosive influence of Western philosophy. So far as nihilism goes, while there might be very few persons that would declare it as a 'path', a way that they follow, our purpose is to show that nihilism in a very general sense arises inevitably from the humanism that now dominates the world, in spite of its pretence of being rational and its claim to support individual self expression while crushing all difference—and all opposition to its uniform values.

The nihilist affirms his own existence, saying, 'I am a nihilist', and at the same time denies that existence through self-identification with 'nothing'. This self-contradictory point of view arises in one sense from narcissism. Denying the Self, the Real, is the last resort of the small self, the 'me', when faced with the impossibility of the narcissistic attitude, which is one of pleasure taken in egoistic self-absorption, and which does not last owing to the impermanence of body and mind upon which it depends. The poet, novelist and playwright Oscar Wilde illustrated this form of self-obsession, so particular to our times, in *The Picture of Dorian Gray*. Dorian, the subject of the portrait, sold his soul so he could stay looking as youthful as he did when his portrait was first painted. As a consequence of living out the decadent theories he had learned from a mentor, he became increasingly morally degenerate. While Dorian showed no visible signs of ageing, the portrait not only aged but also revealed corruption, vanity and cruelty.

The nihilist often begins as an idealist and it has no doubt been well documented in psychological studies how this becomes thwarted so the person turns inward, not in meditation but in vain excesses of self-hatred. For example, here is a statement typical of one that has sought refuge from despair in the deeper despair of nihilism:

> *I have lost all hope and faith in the world and in humanity. Now there is nothing; nothing at all.*

Hope and faith in the world and humanity is the exact reverse of all true spiritual wisdom since time immemorial. So long as we seek happiness in external things, thought to be apart from the Self, we are doomed forever to disappointment.

Tradition has it that if we are kind to humans and other creatures in so far as that is possible and put our faith in God, then we will not be disappointed and we might stand a chance of at least gaining some peace of mind. Oscar Wilde seemed to be showing there are consequences for rejecting this simple exotericism. Existentialism nonetheless puts across the aggressively anti-spiritual notion that there is nothing beyond human existence—by which is meant our experience of that existence or of 'the world' within strictly limited transactional reality. It did this in powerful ways, through literature, art and later, popular music and fashion. At the same time some existentialists fully admitted the absurdity of the premise.

However, the absurdists, having fully accepted the existentialist postulate that *existence precedes essence*, really believed that life itself is without meaning, not suspecting that their idea of 'life' was built upon a mistaken notion, an idea not based on reality but on an empty nothing.[1] 'Existence precedes essence' is the total reversal of metaphysical doctrines of the Real. What was meant by 'existence' is not the equivalent of the Sanskrit *sat*, from *sat-chit-ananda*: being, consciousness and bliss, which is the nature of Brahma, the supreme principle. Existentialism reduces being to common, ordinary human experience and is strictly limited to that, admitting nothing beyond. At the same time, the existentialists wanted to have it that existence, understood in that way, has no conditions, which is certainly absurd! A limit is placed on the universe then this universe is imagined as having no limits. The problem there is that to transcend ordinary human tendencies a superhuman effort is needed, all the more so when it is seen that the effort is to be made from within the strictly limited human domain—even if this is imagined as being unlimited! If existence precedes essence, then we must know that the idea of essence here has nothing to do with the Sanskrit *purusha*, or Atma, as all that has been rejected. It means in this context essential human nature. Finding this depends on extracting an essence out of a being that has no essence other than what can be produced by its own will and actions. Man becomes a faulty demiurge, given an impossible task to perform. Ignorance cannot remove ignorance. Consequently, subsequent existentialist novels and plays often dealt with failure and despair, the inevitable result.

---

[1] Jean Paul Sartre put forward the postulate 'existence precedes essence' in his essay *Existentialism is a Humanism*. By declaring existentialism to be a form of humanism, he aimed to relieve it from the burden of 'pessimism'— though in our view that only placed the final seal on its damnation.

If we pick up any book on existentialism we will probably find the academic view that it is something 'historical'. However, it has become so deeply absorbed into the collective mentality that it no longer matters whether the philosophy itself is even discussed any more. Ironically, while Jean Paul Sartre and his friends declared open war on all tradition, seeing it as 'conformist', the result of the 'lowering of the sky' to exclude everything of a supra-human order was to pave the way for conformity to a degree never seen before. Uniformity is by now the substitute for true unity, which must always depend from a spiritual and natural order.[2]

Nihilism is a philosophical term; Sri Shankaracharya gave it as an example of ignorance fourteen centuries ago. Shankaracharya and his various commentators within the discipline of Advaita Vedanta have pointed out that a certain interpretation of Buddhist texts carries the danger of nihilism. They were referring to the Shunyavada void theory, which declares the absolute non-existence of all things whatsoever. Buddhism is a heterodox *darshana* or school of thought and did not last very long in India, relatively speaking. It went out into the world and proliferated elsewhere. Eventually Buddhism—albeit in a neutered form—became very popular with atheistic psychologists and other material reductionists of the West. The *avatara* Sri Shankaracharya—considered a Jagatguru or 'world teacher', not only a teacher to India—was unambiguous in what he wrote. If he was not in fact denouncing Buddhism he was certainly denouncing an interpretation of it that even then was leading some to nihilism through mistaken denial of the Atma-Brahma principle. On empirical grounds alone there is very good reason for retaining reservations about Buddhism, especially the Westernised forms of it. We have encountered persons throughout our lives that adopted the erroneous void notion. Some of them even thought it represents Advaita Vedanta, so deepening the confusion further. Many of these fell to nihilism, and subsequently to despair and even clinical depression. And all for nothing.

Nihilism really means the denial of the true Self because the ego sense of 'me' is self-evident. Obviously the self exists otherwise who is asking the question or having the thought of nihilism? There is an implicit contradiction in the self-negation. Who is the 'I' in this that likes and dislikes things? Who or what is the 'I' that chooses things and that can affirm and deny them in one breath? Even confusion itself must be separate from the Self. It is no more than an object created by the mind, as is nihilism.

---

[2] See 'Uniformity against Unity', *Thunder Perfect Gnosis*.

Nihilism is a thought comparable to a tiny drop in the great ocean of Brahma. It is like a bubble appearing on the surface of the sea for a moment until it is gone, dissolved back into the water. Shiva drank up all the poisons of the world and turned them into nectar. Christ did the same thing, dying to the body and living in spirit forever for all those that follow him. Kali drinks up all the blood of the universe. This has to be dwelled on constantly and then peace of mind will come—and even much more. Spiritual practice is indispensible and before it is possible we must relinquish all attachments to philosophy in the conventional meaning of that—which should really be strictly limited to the Western philosophers although it is is erroneously used to describe ancient doctrines and their various interpretations. We hope it is fairly obvious we are not making prescription to cure the social and other ills that afflict our civilisation as it nears the end of its time. Non-dual yoga and its preparatory means such as the yoga of the sage Patañjali, which we have written of elsewhere, will only be taken up seriously by a small minority of spiritual seekers. It is those whom we are addressing.

# Qualifications for Advaita

The four qualifications for the path, including the Six Treasures, which are well known to practitioners of Patañjali Ashtanga Yoga, are standard teaching within Advaitan Raja Yoga. The following requirements apply to any serious spiritual path aimed at direct knowledge and not merely religious belief. Here we will go through the qualifications—which are latent within the aspirant and not merely something to be learned—step by step.

**1.** *Viveka*: Ability to discriminate between the real and the seeming or apparent. Knowing the real Self (Atma) from the superimposition.

**2.** *Vairagya*: Dispassion. Freedom from attachment or binding to desires, including likes and dislikes.

**3.** *Shadsampatti*: Literally, 'Six Treasures', which we have given previously, but here they are presented as within Advaita Vedanta:

*Shama*—Mastery of the mind. Calmness; tranquility.

*Dama*—Self-control; mastery of the senses (pleasures in worldly pursuits).

*Uparati*—Mastery of the mind and senses to the extent of being able to concentrate in yoga, or otherwise achieve meditation.

*Titiksha*—Forbearance; being able to withstand the ups and downs of life and everything that life throws at you, whether good or bad.

*Saradha*—Trust (faith) in Vedantic Knowledge; trust in the Preceptor and God. From *saradha* comes *virya*, strength of a special sort.

*Samadhana*—The mind fully concentrated in spiritual Self-enquiry.

**4.** *Mumukshutvam*: Strong desire for freedom from dependence on the world for happiness—which is understood to involve temporary happiness and endless suffering.

*Viveka* is the essential or core practice not only in Advaita Vedanta but also in the Patañjali Ashtanga Yoga. With the latter there is a very detailed method called intellective process, involving identification of five different cognitions (*vrittis*).[3] With Advaitan Non-dual practice, one must first establish all that is the true Self, called Atma, and all that is non-self—all cognitions and perceptions whatsoever, all objects in the universe we perceive as 'out there' and separate from us.

---

[3] See *Thunder Perfect Gnosis*, Part Two.

First we must understand that we are not the body, the primary identification. The body is an object of perception like anything else. This will be looked at in more detail in the chapters that follow. Once that has been clearly established and understood, we can separate our identification with the mind. We tend to think of ourselves as a mind that is inside of a body somehow. Advaita proves it to be false. The mind produces objects based on the senses of hearing, feeling, sight, taste and smell. From this is produced our entire (false) idea of what we call reality. Body and mind undergo constant change. We are born, we are young, we grow older, and eventually the body dies. The body is not therefore Atma, changeless, eternal, and immortal. The mind also undergoes constant change. We know a great deal more than we did when we were a child; we see things differently over time. The mind is not Atma, unchanging, undying, absolute. We *experience* all this: the body growing old, the mind having thoughts, feeling, memories, hopes and fears and so forth. It is the same Atma, called the Witness (a noun not a verb), that is ever-present when we are born and when we die, and that continues afterward and forever, without beginning or end. Atma does not act or participate in the dream or the waking state, or the dreamless deep sleep. Yet It is present, even in that deep sleep when the mind is completely absent and bodily awareness is shut down too.

Our purpose is to know the real, Atma, and to loosen the grip that body and mind has on us, persuading us that 'this body', 'this mind', is the Self, which is false. Knowing this is the *viveka* discrimination, an ongoing enquiry (*vichara*). It is the first qualification for Advaita Vedanta; for without this understanding, at least intellectually, no further progress can be made.

*Vairagya*, 'dispassion', comes about once it is known that we are truly the Atma and all else is non-self. In the meantime it can be practiced. All that we like and dislike has a powerful hold on us, binding us to body and mind so we identify with physical objects and mentality, including feelings and emotions. This does not mean that we no longer experience emotions and thoughts; it means that we know that none of this is the real Self and that it has no absolute reality, only a seeming (or false) reality in the causal world.

*Shadsampatti* is the Six Treasures, essential to practice and the attainment of knowledge of the Real. Control of mind is needed for yoga, not only in one hour of the day but at all times. Calmness and tranquility is cultivated, otherwise meditation is impossible.

From *Viveka* and *Vairagya*, *Shama* and *Dama*, control of mind and senses must come about. So it will now be seen that with the four qualifications and the Six Treasures, each stage arises from the preceding one. Note that control of mind is put first and control of senses comes second. In the case of the ignorant person, the mind follows the senses, upon which it forms objects of perception. So the mind must be controlled before there is any chance of controlling the senses, which are otherwise like wild horses. The senses will then follow the command (will) of the mind and not the other way round. As according to the sage Vyasa,

> Just as bees follow the course of the queen bee and rest when the latter rests, so whenever the mind stops the senses also stop their activities.[4]

The nature of the mind is volatile. One must understand that the mind's engagement with the external or sensory world is twofold: firstly, it flows outward in its hunger to receive impressions. The mind is in fact shaped by these impressions, when it dwells upon them—that alone ought to be enough to prove the importance of the control of mind! Secondly, the mind wishes to impress itself upon the external world; it does this by means of its faculties of action.[5] All of this, both the inflow and the outflow of mind, has its basis in the impulse to be in contact with the external world. A person who cannot control this urge at all will not be able to do yoga, for their mind is continuously flowing outward—they cannot turn the tap off.[6] The one that has even a little control will be able to strengthen that through doing the practice. In regard to this control, it cannot be something that is only done once in a while. It must be continuous, and not only in the one hour of the day when we do a meditation *sādhana* (practice).

---

4 Vyasa's comment on *Yoga-Sutra* 2: 54.

5 The faculties of perception are called Jnana-indriyas. The faculties of action are called Karma-indriyas.

6 At all times when we use the term 'yoga' we refer to Raja Yoga, whether of the Patañjali school or the Advaitan school. It should be noted here that there are degraded forms of yoga that are very popular, usually called 'yoga for health' or something like that. But whatever it is called, and completely unknown to practitioners and teachers alike, it is potentially injurious to the being. Why is this? Yoga was developed thousands of years ago to act as a support for spiritual realisation, which has nothing to do with 'wellbeing' or bodily health alone. Even when yoga is done in ignorance of its true principles, a subtle effect can come about. In the unprepared person, even a spiritual influence, let alone an elemental one of a specific nature, can be harmful owing to the condition of the mind that receives it.

It should be added that the novice will frequently complain that 'something came up' that required their immediate attention. Of course, if we have to attend to an emergency then so be it. Most often than not, however, one thing comes up and then another because the person does not practice self-control. It is no use waiting until all conditions in the world are calm before doing yoga, because that will never come about! It has to be the other way round. First practice control, and then calmness will come about. Until the channels of communication with the world, the inflow and outflow, are closed, then the world will always exert power over the mind and not vice versa.

*Uparati* is called *pratyahara* 'withdrawal of senses' in yoga. That is, the senses are withdrawn from their usual sense objects so that concentration (*dharana*) is possible. In Patañjali Yoga this means concentration of the mind on any object chosen for meditation; in Advaita, this means that the mind sees every object as Brahma, and is absorbed wholly in Brahma. When the level of control is powerful enough and can be sustained then real meditation (*dhyana*) is possible. A translator has mentioned that such control is an activity in itself, though not an activity of the mind as such.[7] This places the practitioner under strain. Such strain is only alleviated by constant practice–that is the point. Eventually the control will become the natural attitude to adopt. Until then, it takes effort.

Furthermore, the conditions of the world are such that there is at all times some force or other exerted on the body. That cannot be stopped, as it is part and parcel of having a body in the first place. Our bodies are subject to heat and cold, hunger and thirst, pain and pleasure and so forth. We can only overcome this if we recollect at all times that 'I am not this body; I am not this mind'. The mind and the body are instruments but must not be confused with the true Self. In that way, it is possible to withstand these external forces and even to ignore them altogether. The next virtue naturally follows this:

*Titiksha* is the ability to withstand everything that life throws at us, all the ups and downs—for it is to be assured that life will present us with continual obstructions to the practice of Self-Realisation. What we see as 'good' or happy things can present as much of an obstacle as what we see as 'bad' or woeful things.

---

[7] *Aparokshanubhuti* with translation and notes by Sri Jnanananda Bharati Swamiji [Vidya Bharati Press].

If we practice *Vairagya* then these will not be such formidable obstructions as they might be otherwise. We will continue the practice no matter what. *Titiksha* is attained when we no longer worry over things, allowing ourselves to enjoy the triumphs and to wallow in regrets over wrong actions or thoughts. Thus if we should fail in *Titiksha*, there is no use in entering into a fight. We must take it back to the first step, *Vairagya*, 'dispassion' or 'indifference' and build up strength again. One must recollect that Atma is the Witness, the observer, and is entirely unaffected by anything. So that we can sustain this, we need the next of the Six Treasures:

*Saradha* is faith in this knowledge, this Non-dual path, and that must involve faith in God and the guru or qualified teacher. Faith already implies knowledge latent and from this comes the powerful spiritual strength called *virya*. Without *Saradha* there can be no *virya*. Such faith does not here imply 'blind faith', as is sometimes the requirement in exoteric religion—but it is only by following out what is prescribed by the guru that the *sadhaka* can test what is said and written against his own experience. Then the knowledge is made strong. What is meant here is by no means theoretical; it is to be based on practical experience. 'Firmness of faith' is also a meaning of *bhakti*, the devotional path.

With *Samadhana* an advanced level has been reached as it is described as 'the mind fully concentrated in spiritual Self-enquiry'. It will not be necessary by now to point out that the Self here has nothing to do with the mind, the emotions, or an exploration of one's psyche or psychology. It is continual engrossment in Atma, the Real. It is also one-pointedness of mind, and with the path of the Non-dual, this means continual absorption in the Real, Atma. What is important to remember here is that the goal must never be forgotten. At this stage, there is little or no desire at all for other things—for that should have been eliminated in the previous practices.

*Mumukshutvam* is the strong desire for liberation or deliverance from the bondage of the world and all the desires for the world, which is called *moksha*. Most especially, from *Viveka* and *Vairagya*, desire for the world is weakened and desire to know the Real is made stronger and stronger—one must maintain a practice of course. Sometimes this last of the four qualifications is translated in the form of a prayer: 'How and when is it to be, O Lord?' This arises from the dissatisfaction with the world, seeing that all attachments lead only to bondage and more suffering. Thus the one that intensely desires liberation yearns not for a condition that might come about in the future, he wants deliverance here and now.

9

# How do we Know?

The complaint often arises that words, by their very nature, are strictly limited when it comes to conveying non-perceptible reality. For instance, we say 'Atma' or 'Brahma', but how do I know what that means if I do not see Brahma? This is very true in so far as the words alone cannot convey what is really meant by them. If a person has never heard the word AUM before then we can show them the writing of the Sanskrit monosyllable. They say, 'Very nice; it looks like a figure three with a crescent and a dot. But what does it mean?' We can say, 'You can also see it as a bow and arrow. The bow is your self, which you imagine to be body and mind. The hand that draws back the bow—an action that requires some effort—is the will to know. The arrow is light or consciousness itself, which must here be directed back to the source of all consciousness, which is called Brahma. When the arrow reaches the goal Brahma is truly known.'

All the same, the person goes away and in the confusion of their mind they think 'Now I know that Brahma is a bow and arrow, which is another word for the same thing. But all I know is words, words and more words! I still do not know Brahma.' That is very true and so for this reason we have a whole range of practices. Even the Advaita Vedanta school, which is not overly concerned with teaching yoga or breathing exercises and so forth, admits that practice is needed and can never be dispensed with until the person realises they are a Jivanmukta, totally enlightened and free forever—here and now, not in some remote future. That is the third and final stage. It is the other two stages we are mostly concerned with here, however much beginning students love to imagine they can get straight to the ultimate goal in 'one flash of light'. In fact, that flash of light experience is very often still an experience and it is not the supreme realisation. The beginner is the one who hears or reads these words and doubts their truth. All the same, he is a beginner, which means he wants to start something, so there is certainly a small part of the *viveka* discrimination in him that thinks 'There might be something in all this'. For him, it is very, very difficult to know how to approach something like Atma, however it is put to him. The practices therefore are really only there to support this knowledge but they are indispensible to beginner and the yogin alike. Of the advanced practitioner, the vision of St. Paul on the road to Damascus is a good example. In one flash of light he saw the truth and simultaneously realised his mission to teach it.

While that experience as such may or may not be the supreme realisation—we cannot really know—it is evident from the writings of St. Paul that his knowledge went to a very high degree.[8] We do not have to be like St. Paul to know with certainty that all these words like Atma, Brahma and so forth, indicate what is real and true. That it is not a mere philosophical puzzle for those who like 'abstract' things. They know all this knowledge, even what is written, is very far from being abstract or 'only in the mind'. In fact, in this day and age, and even a long time ago, those who have reached this level of spiritual maturity are few in number. If you are counted among them then rejoice! You have already received a thousand blessings from the Lord.

The work for the beginner is doing the practice, which means reserving time for it instead of doing and thinking all the other things that can be done and thought about in the (false) world of 'I am this body and mind, in a universe full of other bodies, other minds, creatures and things'. The work for the yogin is to keep on doing the meditation and not to become complacent, thinking it is enough to have a conviction of truth and rest there, or to fall into (tamasic) inertia, as a consequence of neglecting the practice.

Now a word on 'enlightenment', a word that is often used far too loosely: As this knowledge that is our subject is only known with certainty in the minds of a few, what of the further degrees of Self-Realisation—so long as we admit that there are gradations or degrees? It is only in the most rare circumstances that an individual, owing to the accrued *karma* of many previous states of being, has *aparoksha*—direct knowledge of Brahma or the Real through entering what are best termed superconscious states.[9] Of these rare cases, some of them become gurus, and they devise all sorts of ways and means to help others realise what they know with absolute clarity—we are not speaking of a mere philosophical 'solution'.

---

[8] For example, his letters to the Corinthians, reckoned to date from a very early period of Christianity, historically speaking.

[9] This is not 'reincarnation', which is a doctrine of the Theosophists that was invented in the nineteenth century. We refer to the transmigration of souls, which forms an accepted part of nearly all traditions. A soul is not born into a succession of human lives following a timeline forward through 'history'. We are only born and die once in the human state, which is but one of countless states of the being that are possible.

11

It also happens to be true that the various degrees of realisation—while we accept this admittedly dualistic approach to knowledge—owe to the mysterious condition called *maya*, involving, as we have pointed out, previous births. Owing to that, realisation can come to a person at any time, even when it is least expected. This can happen regardless of whether the person seems to 'deserve it' or not, or whether they are thought of, or think of themselves, as being a good or a bad person. In fact, such is the surprise element that St. Paul was a Roman that persecuted early Christians before he 'saw the light' while on the road to Damascus. He went on to become one of the most revered teachers of Christian practice—what a turn around! Metanoia in this case does not only mean changing one's mind about something, it is far more profound and involves real knowledge, not of the ordinary kind.

Multiple errors can arise, which it is our purpose to point out. Firstly, this knowledge is not gained by reading or studies alone, but study is indispensible too as a support to realisation. It is also not even gained by persistent practice—which might come as a surprise to some people, because we know that practice is also indispensible. We could cite examples of persons that were ordained as monks or nuns in certain traditional disciplines—it matters not here of the difference in so-called paths because the goal must always be one and the same no matter how it is named or defined. These did nothing else but study, attend lectures and ordinations and meditate for long hours in isolation. After perhaps as much as fifteen or twenty years, they left the Order and were still in some doubt as to whether God even exists or is real at all—or in the case of Buddhists, many of whom are atheistic, whether there can really be such a thing as is called *nirvana*, and if there is, if it is in any way attainable. Or it may be they doubt if the Buddha himself existed, or avatars in some schools that retain contact with these. These were not in any way changed by what they experienced and before long they forgot most of what they had been doing all those years; what they can remember of it is no different from the recollection of a dream, somewhat vague and ephemeral. However much practice is needed, it is not by practice alone then that Self-Realisation comes about. Individuals are 'qualified' for knowledge in different ways; meditating in a cell or cave for years is no guarantee.

As for those who become Associates or even practitioners of an Order such as ours, they come and go like fish in a pond. If you have ever sat watching fish in a pond for some time then you will know that you see certain fish nibbling around among the weeds. Some of them shoot straight off and disappear. Others stay for a while, or go away and then return, but only a very few actually stay in that one spot you are observing. We will come back to that in a moment. The person that desires more and more sensual enjoyment in life, more 'experience', above all else, will get their wish granted through endless rebirth into other states of being until they realise that the very nature of such desire is never satisfied and leads only to more suffering and death. For the latter, a swift enlightenment will never be gained by 'giving things up' temporarily and then returning to those things as soon as enlightenment is gained, as if it was a bargain! Nothing can be denied until one has really had enough of it all and no longer wants it. To continue the analogy of the fishpond, those who stay in the one spot are as rare as those whom we call 'advanced' because they do not need to have their existence or the existence of God proved to them; they fully intend to take it further than that. If that is their wish then it will be granted sooner or later.

In *Dakshinamurti Stotra* 7: 32, Shankaracharya, different ways of getting to Self-Realisation are mentioned, and by that what is meant is knowing that the true Self is Brahma and no other, sometimes called 'enlightenment'.[10] Firstly, there is the way of Advaita Vedanta, which is directly knowing, seeing or recognising through *viveka* discrimination that Atma and Brahma are truly one. Then there is *smrti* or secondary knowledge, which means diligently studying the *shruti* scriptures and their commentaries, learning, memorising, thinking and meditating on them. This may seem a contradiction of what was said earlier, that real knowledge is not acquired by reading a book, or even hundreds of books. In fact, while the words alone do not convey the knowledge, they point to that which is far beyond the mind to comprehend on its own ground. For this reason, scriptures are valid testimony and by a certain mystery of the Lord of the Universe and the power of Maya for some few persons partial or even full realisation can come about. It serves this way or route to knowledge by positing that Atma is known 'inside the body' (*Bhagavad Gita* 13: 2). While this is not strictly speaking true, for the lesser cannot contain the greater, it is the first step on the road to enlightenment and has been proved over very many centuries to work.

---

[10] *Dakshinamurti Stotra with Manasollasa* [Sri Ramakrishna Math].

There is a kind of intermediary between this second way and the third one, which will be described in a moment. How can the mind know something that is not of the mind? The mind sees objects. The objects themselves are not self-luminous. Does the mind see things with its own light? This can be proved not to be so. The mind itself only exists because of what is called the light of consciousness—one must make a clear difference between thought and consciousness. This self-luminous light—for nothing else can illuminate it—is called the Witness, which observes all but does not participate. That is called Atma, which is one with Brahma. If the mind constantly turns to thoughts of this one light, which is all-pervading consciousness, not of the mind, an impression is formed in the mind that will ultimately erase all other impressions, because although it is still *chitta-vritti* ('stream or wave' of mind), it happens to be true whereas all other impressions are not true. In this way the mind assists in its own sublation. This might also be seen as the real power of the Word, which as according to St. John the Evangelist, is 'with God', and is also called Christ or Krishna or by countless names in all traditions.

Thirdly there is the case of *aparoksha*, the direct experience of realised souls as 'I am Brahma'. These sometimes become gurus with special powers to help them in their mission. The fullest kind of *samadhi* called Nirvikalpa is among what we call superconscious states. This *samadhi* does not require any effort, although the person might have put that effort in towards attainment of more ordinary kinds of *samadhi* for many years. Either way, the recipient must be prepared for such an experience by spiritual practice otherwise it counts for nothing. As this comes about through previous births, as we have said, it is unpredictable. It can come at any time. Nirvikalpa literally means 'without change', which means without mental fluctuations. In fact, it is sometimes compared to being in deep dreamless sleep (*sushupti*) then becoming fully conscious without returning to the dreaming or the wakeful states. It is clearly stated in the *Upanishads* that he who awakens in this way will know Brahma. The mind is hardly present at all, only in a seed form, so to speak. One is not aware of body or mind. How is it then possible to know that we were in deep sleep? Consciousness, the Witness, is Atma, not the mind or the thoughts. In Nirvikalpa we *are* Atma and no other while the mind and body are in a dormant state. We also know that Atma and Brahma are one, as this is self-evident in that *samadhi*. The full Sanskrit word *aparokshanubhuti* for this direct knowledge is translated differently in books and dictionaries but in the highest sense it is 'the self vanishing into Brahma'. Hold on to that thought—it is what is meant by the sublation of the mind.

14

Lastly, there is *aitihya*. This is the oral tradition passed on from guru to the disciples as in *That thou art* (*tat-tvam-asi*), one of the great statements of the *Upanishads*. Put simply, it means that 'you are, in reality, Brahma'. It should be mentioned as we are writing this in the penultimate phase of the Age of Kali Yuga that a disciple has to be exactly that, in the etymological meaning of the word, 'follower of the discipline'. So yes, they follow the guru but that also means they follow out *what he teaches*, including the practical instruction! As a genuine guru is magnetic, in a manner of speaking, with or without special powers of charisma, eloquence and so forth, there will always be those drawn to him but unable to in any way comprehend who or what he truly is—they only see the man. The same is also said of avatars in the *Bhagavad Gita*, that Krishna is able to dwell in a human form from time to time but men will not see Krishna, they only see the human being. In their ignorance of reality, for they only see the covering or superimposition called *maya*, they are quite unable to pass beyond the appearance of things in the world. To the enlightened person they are exactly like prisoners in an iron cage—and they do not see the cage. That cage is the body and the mind, which they accept as absolute reality, no matter what words are said to the contrary in spiritual texts or even by direct word of a guru who has true knowledge of what he is talking about.

The universe of physical objects is to the unenlightened person beyond dispute. In fact, even Advaita Vedanta, the highest knowledge, does not deny that things exist or that we experience those things in our bodies and minds. What it does do is deny them ultimate reality. The most often used analogy is that of the rope hanging in a darkened room that is mistaken for a snake. If someone tells you it is a rope and you look more closely you will see it is a rope, which is the reality. After that, you only see the rope and are not deluded by the appearance of the snake. Now this analogy and others of a similar kind, involving clouds in the sky that appear as castles, creatures or giants, or trees that appear from the distance to be a man, is repeated many times in Advaitan texts, and for good reason. The reason is that no matter how many times it is heard it is very difficult for a person to grasp who believes that their Self (really Atma) is the body and mind, that they have a 'life', consisting of firstly the fact that they were born, then the name that was bestowed on them by parents, then a history of events, situations, triumphs and failures, memories and so forth, along with all they are attached to as possessions, including the relationships of friends, wives, husbands, parents, children, grandchildren and even pet animals, for example.

This powerful belief is reinforced since the day we are born. We learn that we have a name that distinguishes us from others. We have parents; we live in a house, a city, a country and so forth. Then education continues to teach us about objects completely apart from the true Self, even to what is considered to be an advanced level. Everything, even if we study Quantum Physics, is a story of objects apart from ourselves and includes nothing at all about the nature of the Self, called Atma-Brahma. Television, newspapers, media, the talk of other persons, all of it serves to reinforce the great delusion of the separate self involved in a world 'outside' as though it were the supreme reality, beyond argument. Only metaphysics dares to reject this belief, this mistaken identification. There is one other route to enlightenment mentioned specifically in the commentary of Swami Harshananda on 7: 32 of *Dakshinamurti Stotra*, which is that of inference (*anumāna*):

Here, the *jiva* or individual self or ego is realised as not essentially different from Ishvara, God or the Lord of the Universe as it is put in the Vedic *shruti* scriptures. This way is held in common with Advaita and Ashtanga Yoga, though the means to it are different. This last way is very prone to error in those whose minds are faulty. The person says, 'I am God; that's great and so what? Nothing else to do then.' However, in yoga the realisation comes about when the fluctuations or 'waves' (*upadhis*) of the mind and all its various impressions are stilled or suppressed completely. Then there is no difference seen between the reflection of sky in water and the sky itself. This way is mentioned in the *Yoga-Sutras* and it is by no means something that a person will get to by attending a few classes or doing a banishing ritual every day for a few months. Acceptance of it as an ideal in the mind only is also very dangerous, for reasons that should be fairly obvious. The person so deluded may, to a certain extent, spread their delusion to others, acting out a rôle of *anti-guru*. Yet for some of those so taken in by a charlatan—and a charlatan may yet be sincere in his mistaken beliefs—even that encounter might provide a means to realisation so long as they are able to free their minds. Things are never as simple as we might like, however. It may also be that the guru is telling the truth and is absolutely valid. It is only that the person, not willing or able to follow the teaching, or lacking in faith and the intellect to comprehend it, seeks an easy way out of the dilemma by declaring they have seen through the disguise and already have found a greater truth! All such problems, however, arise from belief that the body and mind are the real Self. This is the essential error of all men, even when they need no proof that they exist as it is self-evident.

16

Advaita does not deny existence when it says the world is an illusion. It is pointing to the source of that appearance, which is the sole Real. In that way, all that exists is real also—and one. It must be understood clearly that there are not two things, Maya and the Real. With knowledge the appearance, how things seem to be, vanishes and is replaced by the realisation that nothing exists outside of Brahma.

In the final measure, nothing exists that is apart from light or consciousness, and by now we hope to have established clearly that *light of consciousness* is not the same thing as mind and thought. It remains to mention here a question that persistently arises as soon as we talk of 'enlightenment', which as we have said is used far too loosely, most particularly in popular New Age books and by those with pretended knowledge. It is a mistake to imagine that, as this constitutes a permanent change of state in the being—we never return to a previous state—we will then see the exterior world vanish away or otherwise will see everything in rays of light. No, this is not in any way true, not even of some of the greatest spiritual masters the world has known. The exterior world still looks the same. The difference is that we know that the world is *not*, only Brahma *is*. We do not all have to become monks. But we must become monks *in our hearts*. The realisation is an interior one.

# Enquiry into the Nature of the Self

Advaita Vedanta teaching, if we take the work of the avatar Sri Shankaracharya as the model, is at least 1,400 years old. In fact that is only the written down part, the tradition is at least 5,000 years old. So while some of the principles of this, the most complete and perfect knowledge that is the highest goal of any human being to reach, have been misappropriated by New Age fake spirituality, the core teaching remains impervious to such assaults made upon it. The enquiry into the nature of the true Self, or Atma, is supported by the recognition that 'I am not this body, I am not this mind'. That happens to contradict everything that is 'normally' and habitually assumed to be the self.

The first stage of the work corresponds to *Solve* in alchemy: we have to use *viveka* discrimination to separate out what is not the Real, the Self, from all else. Consciousness is not the same as mind, thoughts or feelings. Adi Shankaracharya gives many examples to prove this by simple logic, which any intelligent person should be able to testify from their own experience. It is not something that has to be believed in, or an abstract philosophy to entertain the mind. The testimony is what we all experience all of the time—it is not some sort of mysticism. But there is a great deal of repetition of these simple examples because it is very hard for people to 'get it'. The person must realise it for themselves and not merely be convinced or persuaded by a powerful argument, or feel they want to believe it. It is very hard for people to grasp that their perceptions, both external and even subtle, or of the mind internally as experience, are not the Real (Atma). To understand this and even to know it or realise it—which is not the same as understanding it though that helps—is a very important step to have reached on the way of Self-Realisation.

How does a person internalise this teaching in such a way that they are able to live out its principles? This cannot be done overnight, much as people would like to have 'instant enlightenment' served up for them on a plate, or on the click of a mouse. We have already covered the four stages in the traditional method. Internalising it means realising it to be true so there is no doubt in the mind. When it comes to living out its principles we are skating on a very thin sheet of ice if we think we can do this before we have achieved actual realisation—which is more than intellectual understanding. Otherwise, if we try to live it out when our basis is imperfect knowledge and insufficient preparation, purification of mind and so forth, we will fall flat on our faces. Others will not be fooled by our pretension.

If it is 'lived out' only in exterior ways—something implied by the very terms we have chosen here—then it has become something very different from Self-Realisation in the way it is meant here, and there is no truth involved. It contradicts the first limb of the Ashtanga Yoga. Until realisation is gained, what we think of as 'my life', 'how I live', always brings us back to the ignorance of 'my self is this body, my self is this mind', which means automatically there are all these other selves and objects out there in the world that are *not* my Self. That automatically evokes fear—fear of all those things that are not my self. I like this but I hate that. 'I am what I like' automatically evokes all we dislike. All induces fear.

Until realisation is fully gained, then living out principles is usually about ordinary things. It boils down to morality and ethics. We can only 'do the right thing', 'do what seems to be best', or do things that do not cause harm to others, as stated in the Eight Limbs of Yoga for example. That is all about doing and action, which is *karma*. The way of Self-Realisation is not about doing things and acting as such. The realisation is internal not external. But that does not mean that when we gain realisation, or even enlightenment, we stop doing anything in the world at all. We will continue to do what we have to do but we will see things very differently. We will no longer be lost in *samsara*, the world illusion.

We need to be clear on this however: the first two steps of the Eight Limbs of Yoga, *yamas* and *niyamas*, cannot be missed out. Otherwise doing yoga is like a man with no legs trying to stand up. It is impossible. Once we have got the basis, then we can go to the yoga, *samadhi* and the way of Self-Realisation in earnest. However, if at the very beginning of practice we want to make it all about doing things and acting then we fail in the concentration within, which is necessary before meditation is even possible. Such ideas about external things will prevent us from doing the practice—it leads us outside of and away from the Self and into the exterior world, which includes thoughts, fears and imagining. The purpose of the first two limbs, 'abstentions and practices', is to get all that out of the way—it does not become an end in itself. If that happens then the clear water of a practice well done is turned into mud straight away and we cannot see a thing, because of the mental habit of putting everything outside the Self through self-identification with exterior objects. It is the most common error in the world. We could even say it belongs to the world but not to the Self. This is why we need to work the first stage in Self-Realisation, which is to use *viveka* discrimination to separate out everything that is not the real Self and establish ourselves in the Atma Self, at least intellectually.

19

That might seem like a contradiction but otherwise it is all mixed up and any practice will be ineffective so it is not even worth doing in the first place.

The conservation of energy for the Great Work is frequently not understood at all by practitioners, or if it is understood, as soon as they get immersed in the world—which is in most cases nearly all the time—they slip back helplessly into the 'default mode' of worldly people and forget the true Self. Logistics, problem solving and all that, there is no end to it. Then they spend an entire day involved with appointments, tasks, meetings and so on, and they try to diligently put in twenty minutes or so yoga and meditation practice the last thing before they go to bed at night, by which time the body and mind are tired and all they really want to do is sleep. In that case, to use a sacrificial analogy, all we are doing is offering the dregs or leavings, and keeping the good wine for chats and tasks and appointments and all the rest of it. We have to sort out what we have to sort out, but if we do it that way we are losing ourselves in 'ordinary life' and forgetting that we are Atma, infinite.[11] That is the whole point of doing the *viveka* discrimination.

So much misery arises when we grasp and try and hold on to exterior things, which is always in the hope of finding joy and happiness. But if we do that, the pleasures are only temporary and we are taken along with the ups and downs, and the unavoidable woes and sorrows when expectations are unfulfilled. This applies to everything in life: relationships, husband, wife, children, possessions, even pet animals and cars, houses, money, status, our achievements and failings, all of it. We try and find happiness in things that are not permanent. It will bring nothing but endless misery and all because we were trying to find happiness in other people and things and not looking for that happiness within that is unchanging and forever. Then we get old and it does not get better. When we die all of it is gone—and death is the one certain truth that no one can argue against.[12] What then of our achievements and failings, joys and sorrows, our possessions and responsibilities? All gone.

---

[11] The term 'ordinary life' is explained in 'Tiger of Fear'.

[12] In fact there have been and perhaps still are 'immortalists' that think that the immortality referred to in scriptures, alchemical texts and so forth, can be gained literally in the flesh. These tend to lose credibility when they die!

When we are able to find that deep spiritual joy from knowledge within we can still act in the world as necessary but if we know our Self is Brahma, infinite, then what more do we need? We have everything we could possibly want. It can then easily be seen that possession of anything is an illusion, even if it is a very powerful illusion for most people. All the same that does not mean we have to 'give up' all our possessions to follow out a spiritual path, or go to live in a cave in the Himalayas, or join a monastery. The realisation is internal not external. From that perspective it makes no difference whether we live in a shed, a caravan or trailer, or a billionaire mansion surrounded by trees—and no doubt electronic security fences and surveillance cameras.

The enlightened person does not self-identify with all these exterior objects any more than the objects of mind, because they know that their Self is in reality infinite, absolute Brahma, the 'one without a second'. That can never be changed. The billionaire who is in ignorance of the true Self is still subject to fears and worries and one day will get old and suffer sickness and then death. So much for the billionaire mansion. Someone else has it now. It may be passed on to children but we do not experience the 'future' through children or other people. The best thing to pass on to children is knowledge and even that is very difficult when they are brought up in a modern world that will completely overwhelm them with powerful arguments against all spiritual reality. All the rules and obligations of 'ordinary life' we have touched on here are referred to *samsara* or the great world illusion as it is termed. But that does not mean we can duck out of the inevitable responsibilities. We will see things differently, however. The person that is lost in all those worries and cares and duties and things in the world, that imagines it all to be his Self, which is called *avidya*, 'not seeing' or ignorance, is lost in *samsara*. He is described as a beast of burden.[13] He worries that he should have done this or that. 'Why did I do this when I should have done that?' It goes on forever, without end. Seeing it all for what it truly is, even knowing our Self as the infinite, absolute, pure being, consciousness and bliss at all times, will not make the world go away. When we come out of meditation, even if we have reached the level called Nirvikalpa Samadhi, the highest, the world of things will be the same old world. Even God or Ishvara, the Lord of the Universe, does not put an end to this world until the time comes to put an end to it. It is not something that comes about through our own efforts.

---

[13] *Upanishads* and texts and commentaries of Shankaracharya.

Managing our lives then, which takes so much of our time, is not a spiritual thing and it can never be that because 'my life' is exterior. So we do the best we can with all of that. However, the full interior realisation *does* alleviate suffering. The person that has no belief in God or Reality other than body and mind suffers a great deal. The people they know and love will die and eventually they will die too, and they think it is like switching off a television set, nothing else to it. That is very, very miserable, and from the point of view of the Brahma-jnanin person, it is in itself a matter of some sorrow to see people suffer like that and not be able to help them because they are materialists that hate religion, God and real spirituality. But that is also their 'choice'. If it is the *karma* of the yogin to help other people then he is not deluded into thinking he can do very much to help people like that apart from in ordinary ways such as is done by charities—feeding and clothing the poor, providing shelter for the homeless. The yogin that follows the way of being a teacher to others will concentrate on helping those ones who can be helped because they have not destroyed the knowledge of the Real that is always inside them. As for the rest he practices forbearance and the Six Treasures, and so far as harmful or evil people are concerned, total indifference. There is one other way for the enlightened person that we shall come to at the end of this.

Practice is reading the right materials and thinking on it a great deal, as we have said. Then the meditation, over time, brings about realisation gradually. Other things can take care of themselves; or when it is something we have to take care of then we must do what is needed but we do not worry about all the rest. In meditation the mind is completely stopped and one idea is held in the heart-mind— ego awareness is theoretically located in the 'cave' inside the heart lotus, which is called the Seat of Brahma. Even doing that for ten minutes a day can make a huge difference so long as we are studying and thinking on the path as much as we can for all the rest of the time. Even in meditation intellect is needed—but it is a different kind of intellect, and not what people usually think of as intellect. What we refer to here is more like a flow of pure knowledge. Even reflected consciousness (the I-sense in Patañjali yoga) is not thought.

From a dualistic point of view—yet it is one that can take us very far—wisdom is an authentic relationship, as is the relation between the guru and the *chela*. Abiding with what is Real or True at the deepest level is not a relationship though, because it is realised as your Self and there is no other. Brahma is one without a second, which is Advaita Non-duality.

In the meantime, we can use a lot of duality and sometimes the yoga of devotion (*bhakti*) is considered the highest path—and that is when the person realises the Self and the Real and still wants to go on loving God (in whatever name and form) out of the sheer joy. It is called 'auspicious' in the scriptures. That is why we include *bhakti* in the wide range of our Raja Yoga practices, as well as the Advaita Non-dualism we are here discussing, which is the highest knowledge.

Lastly, a question frequently made by the unenlightened person is 'What is the point?' Meaning, 'If I should become enlightened then what can I do with that?' We will ignore the obvious case where the person is just thinking about wanting something other than pure knowledge—which automatically means no enlightenment because whenever there is a lack or a need then ignorance is there too. Desire for knowledge is acceptable, though. So far as post-enlightenment goes, if we can use such bizarre terms (considering the subject itself), there are three ways: the first way is that the person renounces everything and vanishes into the infinite. This is perfectly fine—all this depends on *karma*. It is only dangerous to try and do something that amounts to the *karma* of another person. The second way is that the person stays around to help other people in the way of knowledge—they defer their retirement from the world in that way.

The third way is that the person works to help others in material ways, as with charities, good works and so forth. None of that can bring knowledge to the unenlightened or to the doer of the good works. When an enlightened person does that he does not seek anything for himself. His involvement with the world does not mean he is lost in that world. He is forever and always with the Self, which is called Brahma or Brahma consciousness. So there are three ways of non-action and action—and all of them are in reality 'actionless action'.

# Question of the Knower

The question and the questioner are one question: 'Who am I?' All questions of the truth rest on the knowledge of the nature of the Self. The traditional method of discourse between guru and *chela*—or the doubter, as it may be—is set down here.[14] It is taken for granted that the beginner will have studied the scriptures, of which the most well known in Hinduism is the *Bhagavad Gita*. Studying does not mean reading the first two chapters and leaving it there! The advice to students is to repeat back in your own words some of what you have read without changing the meaning. Then reflect on it, and consider if it is true in relation to your experience. When doubts remain, formulate your questions and put them to the teacher. He will then explain further, on that basis, in an attempt to dispel the doubts. Once doubts are dispelled, the person may take up the practice of meditation, which is to strengthen and internalise the knowledge thus gained.

Nonetheless, this method of question and answer is reasoning, and of course it cannot be guaranteed that all doubts are removed. With Advaita Vedanta, no one is asked to believe anything but to consider it carefully. The difficulty that everyone has with Advaitan Non-dualism is that it deals with a lot of things we normally take for granted and never question. Once it is considered to be true, or even that 'I have a feeling it might be true', then it can be meditated on, because that feeling or sense of the presence of truth has a germ of knowledge within it. Following here are some of the questions that arise whenever Advaita Vedanta is open to general discussion. The questions are fairly typical of beginners, yet even practitioners that have followed a discipline of meditation for some time sometimes will find that such doubts arise to disturb their meditation.

**Q.** Advaita says that perceptions and experience are unreal. I find this difficult!

**A.** The statement requires some qualification. Advaita declares that perceptions and experience are not *ultimately* real. They are still real enough in the world of cause and effect, which we perceive with mind and senses, cognition. The difference to make is primarily between the seer and the seen:

---

[14] A *chela* (Sanskrit) is one that follows a guru, 'one that is eager to learn'. The follower may also have doubts. The guru will dispel all doubt but clearly that does not apply to the sceptic, who wishes only to argue.

24

You see a cup, glass or other vessel. How do you see it? With your eyes. Do your eyes really see it, the physical organs? No, the eyes are the physical instruments but you see it in your mind with the inner sense of sight: your mind forms a picture of it and you recognise it by its name and form. Is the cup or glass self-luminous? No, your mind has illuminated it and what you see is a sensory impression. This is called an object. You then think, 'I know this'. But where is the 'I'? You will never think 'I am that cup', so you know for certain that the cup is separate from your Self. What then is it that illuminates the mind—that gives the mind the power to form impressions of objects that seem to be exterior? The first part is easy but the second part is harder. Does the mind know itself? The answer (from Advaita) is no. All the mind does is reflect on its own thoughts by creating other thoughts and impressions.

**Q.** Then how do we know we have a mind? How do we experience what we are experiencing in our minds?

**A.** Close your eyes and stop your thoughts even for a few seconds. Even though you are not having thoughts, memories or impressions of things, objects, experiences, *something* is experiencing the sense of 'I'. You know that you exist even without thoughts because you can stop them at least for a few seconds. So you know you are not your body because your mind sees and feels that as an object. Now you know that you are not your mind either. This is the next step towards Self-Realisation. It makes becoming a practitioner possible.

Some further examples: when you go to sleep and dream you are not aware of your body but your mind continues to form sensory impressions. You can dream you are in China but when you wake up you know you never left your bed. It was a dream and yet it seemed completely real at the time. The mind can create an entire world, with time, memories and all sorts of subtle things. When you pass into deep sleep, which most people do and it is certainly needed otherwise we get exhausted, there are no dreams. Where are you then? When you wake up, you say 'I was in deep sleep without dreams and I remember nothing but I feel better for that good sleep'. Your mind and body were not there, the body shut down, the mind not functioning—and yet you can still wake up. The world has not disappeared and 'you' are still there. What is it that knows this? Put it another way: through that dreamless oblivion what was it that was still there, knowing the absence of mind and body? This is more difficult for most people to understand but here it is:

Atma is the true Self. Atma is the Witness, the Seer that is at all times self-luminous. The mind is only able to shine in that light—the mind is not self-luminous. Atma is self-luminous. Atma is the real Self but we mistake it for mind and body all the time. It is like the reflection in a mirror. How do we know we have a face? We can only see our face in a mirror. We only see our eyes in a mirror and yet we think the eyes see things. Actually we see things in our mind, which is the instrument of knowing perceptible things, both gross (physical) and subtle (in a dream or otherwise imagined). The ignorance of thinking we are body and mind is like thinking we are the reflection in the mirror and there is nothing that is being reflected. That is the ordinary state of affairs that Advaita Vedanta seeks to remove. Only knowledge destroys ignorance—and we need our minds for that!

Saying, 'I am not this mind; I am not this body' is to remove the false identification between the real Self and the mind and body. It does not mean you will stop having a body and a mind while you are still living. You experience the body as an object; you can see it and feel it. But the body does not see and feel things on its own. The mind too is an object—it is not self-luminous. It is illuminated by what is called the Self, the Atma, Witness, Seer, and Knower. Atma does not participate in action but it is there forever. It is pure consciousness. The I-sense (ego) and mind borrow that light to form impressions, which are mistakenly thought to be the real Self. So when you say, to remove the false identification and help to know the real Self as Atma, 'I am not this mind; I am not this body', that does not mean you will make the mind and body disappear. They are still there. There are still people on the street outside. The Moon still rises in the East. There are stars in the sky. The car park fills up at certain times of the day.

**Q.** Supposing I have to deal sometimes with angry or even violent people. How does spiritual consciousness help with that?

**A.** Being illuminated or in spiritual consciousness does not mean that other people will stop getting angry and violent. But *you* will stop getting angry and violent and as a rule you will be peaceful and calm (*sattvic*) more of the time, whatever is going on. Angry people are scared people. They are very fearful. All fear results from egoism, which arises from what Advaita calls ignorance. The ignorance (and fear) arises precisely from that sense of separate existence as 'I, myself'—the feeling that we are a little person in a vast world full of other people, creatures and things that are completely separate.

Fear arises from that unknown, the sense of self as a separate existence. A totally illuminated person does not fear things because they know all of it is an appearance of—their Self. Yes, really! All those angry, mad people are really an appearance of your true Self, through the projecting power of Maya, the weaver of all world appearance, no other than Brahma supreme. We were giving the very high example previously. But first we have to pass through the stage of *viveka* discrimination where we see everything that is non-self, the appearance, the mind and body, and remember constantly the real Self as the Witness, the shining illuminator of all things, and without which nothing could exist at all: Atma, infinite, absolute, never born, never dying and self-luminous. Atma is not an object—all else is an object.

**Q.** How does one bring truth into the world?

**A.** There is more than one answer to a big question like that. Starting with the high end: truth is already everywhere in the world in so far as the world is an appearance of the ultimate reality, Brahma, all-pervading. So we do not need to bring truth into the world because the world already *is* that. We only have to realise it for a fact. Then Self-Realisation amounts to the same, no difference, because Atma (Self) and Brahma (Universal) are one and not two things. Self-Realisation does not bring truth into the world; it brings the realisation of the truth that is already everywhere and that has always existed. It is there now and it always will be for all of time. Quite often in the background of this question is a secondary item, which we will deal with next:

**Q.** Why is there evil in the world?

**A.** The simple answer is ignorance (*avidya*), which then brings us back to the previous: only knowledge (*jnana*) destroys ignorance. The veil upon the truth is then lifted and truth is seen everywhere. The next question really follows on the same lines:

**Q.** How does one bring truth into being?

The last three questions arise when a person is very concerned about the external conditions they find in the world. There is so much unhappiness and misery. Some persons do not let this bother them much at all, they are very engrossed in their idea of their self in relation to a world they think is separate from them. They are only concerned with their achievements, triumphs and—sometimes—their perceived errors and shortcomings! The differences between persons are as waves upon the water. No wave is identical to another but all are made of water. In Advaita, that is called the Sea of Brahma.

A person that has greater spiritual maturity will be concerned by the fact of suffering in the world. They will naturally want to make the world a better place. However, this question is already answered when we know that truth is everywhere but we have to realise it, see it and know it for a fact. The word 'being' calls to mind the fact that the entire universe seems to be full of exterior objects but in reality the universe is *being*. God, Ishvara or whatever we want to call it, is Pure Being at what appears to be the causal level from the individual point of view. Brahma is *sat-chit-ananda*—pure being, consciousness and bliss, infinite, absolute. It is already true so there is nothing we can do to make it true. We only have to realise it as fully as possible. Realising it fully is the highest goal for a human being to achieve, as stated in the Vedas.

**Q.** How does enlightenment show up in the world if not through action?

**A.** That question could also be framed as an objection! Our world—really the Western world or the kind of idealism that governs that—is very much oriented towards action. This is even pushed to the extent where action is valued above all else. The answer from Advaita is the complete opposite of that: action (*karma*) cannot destroy ignorance; it cannot bring about knowledge or enlightenment. Not even good actions can do that, as we may judge them to be. Only knowledge destroys ignorance. Knowledge is not action. Knowledge is in reality much closer to *being* as we previously mentioned. We are what we know, not what we see or think.

**Q.** How then can people be helped?

**A.** It needs to be established first that not everyone can be helped. Sometimes it is harmful to us to try to help those who will not be helped—for all sorts of reasons. Sometimes it is even harmful to the person being 'helped', for example in the wrong way or through ignorance. Unless we are omniscient, we cannot possibly know and understand the totality of *karma* that brought that person into life as a human being. The idea of action in the world comes into this again: action does not bring enlightenment; this has to be remembered. If we see someone fall down in the middle of a busy road we can go and pull them out to save them from injury but that will not enlighten the person we have rescued or us. Some people that are very concerned about the suffering in the world set up places or organisations where food is provided for the hungry, shelter for the homeless, for example. This is all very good but it does not bring enlightenment to anyone.

Also, if we see a homeless person on the street it is well not to think we are better than them if we have a nice comfortable house and enough money to keep us. They are still an appearance of God in the world. There is nothing that can exist outside of God (or Brahma). It makes sense then to treat other people and creatures with respect and as well as we can.

There is a dangerous aspect to the same question. While wanting to help people or make the world a better place is essentially honourable—and most people will see it as honourable—such a motivation can secretly arise from a desire to be liked, admired and respected by other people. That is egoism, arising from the same ignorance as we have been discussing. From the Advaitan perspective it is no better than wanting to be hated by other people. All of that is to be lost in *samsara* (world illusion)—thinking the Self to be separate from all else. It is to think that we lack something, we need something or that we are missing something—that we are somehow incomplete. In reality, we already have everything—without owning or possessing it. We only have to realise that. There is a further aspect of this question, whether asked directly or not:

**Q.** What is the use of knowledge then?

**A.** This question is also very much in the way of an objection! We hope to have already shown what is the point of it all, but there is a further consideration: when a person does real meditation, even if they are in a cave far away from anyone, some of that *sattvic* light goes out into the world. It is a mistake to think that the actionless action of meditation cannot improve things for humanity as a whole. It is a mistake to think that only external action can be helpful. The thought that only external action can be helpful is itself born of the ignorance of imagining that the Self (Atma) is the body and mind from which action is born; from those actions other actions are born, and on and on indefinitely (*karma*).

**Q.** How can objective reality be merely an object of the mind?

**A.** Firstly a qualification is needed. Objective reality actually consists of countless millions of objects and not just one object. We can also call that 'relative reality', as pertaining to the empirical level. We experience all of that in our minds. Take away the mind and there is no objective reality for us to know about. It is also self-evident from a few moments thought that we only experience it in our minds. Advaita does not deny there is a thing called objective or empirical reality. It only denies that it has *ultimate* reality.

It is self-evident, according to this teaching, that we experience objective reality but that is also called ignorance—because it is only taken as real by the being that does not know the true state of affairs. Knowledge of the real destroys the illusion. This is often compared to the analogy of the rope mistaken for a snake. A rope hanging in a darkened room can be mistaken for a snake—it is how it appears. But when it is known to be a rope the person no longer sees the snake. Are there two things, rope and snake? No. In reality there is only the rope. This question often gives rise to another:

**Q.** So the world is only there because I imagine it?

**A.** Yes and no. It is only there because you experience it in your mind but you are not a demiurge God. When we die, the world does not stop existing but we will not see it anymore or experience it.[15] The world—whether we see it or not—is the product of Maya, without beginning or end. Maya cannot be explained from within *maya*, the appearance otherwise called the world illusion. Maya has two powers: projecting Brahma as an appearance and covering or hiding the Real. These two powers are really one and the same. Maya does this through Name and Form. According to Advaita, 'matter' cannot be its own cause or the cause of anything subtler. The entire universe is Consciousness in reality. It starts there.

**Q.** What is the notion of the intellect in meditation? It appears to be different from what is usually supposed.

**A.** Mind and intellect, as regarded technically in meditation, are not the same thing. There are two essential approaches to meditation in Ashtanga Yoga. Firstly, there is meditation upon an object, whatever that may be, with the purpose of engrossment in that, eventually transcending name and form. When that happens the object is realised to be something that is made perceptible by the mind. The second approach involves meditation without an object, with the primary goal of engrossment in pure self-awareness, the pure I-sense (ego).[16] What is being described is still reflective consciousness, not the Atma consciousness itself—although Atma or *purusha* (as it is termed in the *Yoga-Sutras*) is always the goal. Between the Atma and the I-sense awareness is the seat of what is called the intellect in yoga and Advaita, the *boddhi*. This *boddhi* is not within the individuality: the individual sense of 'I' is a *product* of this higher intellect, a modification of it. Below that again is the mentality, which consists of further degrees of modification.

---

[15] We cannot go into the question of postmortem states here.

[16] The primary goal but not the final or ultimate goal by any means!

The mind is assisted by its ten faculties of action and sensation, by which objects are formed. Such objects can be either exterior, such as a tree, a pot. Or they can be interior (subtle) such as an imagined tree or pot. Going back up the ladder of the five envelopes of being (as they are called), and arriving back at the I-sense (second rung from the top): When thought is stopped, as in Samyama Yoga, then the ray of light from *boddhi* is directly perceived in the I-sense. This enables a special kind of knowledge of any object that is being meditated on. This is more than ordinary knowledge. For example, if we want to know science we need to read a science book. If we want to learn about history we read history. That is ordinary knowledge and it is indirect—it rests on inference. The special knowledge is the real essence of that thing, which is beyond name and form. It is called *pratyaksha* as the highest form of direct cognition and beyond that, *aparoksha*, which is beyond sensory cognition altogether. This question always raises a further one:

**Q.** What then is meditation?

**A.** Answering the question as to what meditation is would of course require at least a small book, and we have written several. Here we are only dealing with the question within the context of some previous questions that have been put here. Firstly what it is not. It is never about sitting quietly and being introspective. Sitting quietly and being introspective can sometimes be efficacious, especially if it is more in the way of contemplation, where the mind is relaxed but is nonetheless focussed on one thing. That is not meditation (*dhyana*) though. Meditation is only possible when concentration of the mind (*dharana*) is accomplished along with withdrawal of the senses from their usual sense objects (*pratyahara*). So real yogic meditation, while requiring peace, calmness and tranquility so the mind is not in any way agitated, is nonetheless an intense inward activity, and this might also be called intellectual activity. But that is very different from the common or garden notion of 'intellectual', which implies having a lot of thoughts about something, or otherwise a kind of abstraction, which yoga never is as the concern is always knowledge of real things or reality Itself.

**Q.** Is there a deeper arcanum behind the simple teaching as put here?

**A.** The deeper arcanum and the simple teaching are one and the same thing—in Advaita there cannot be one thing and another thing. The simplest of truth is the deepest, the most profound when truly known or 'experienced'—that is, from the point of view of the individual that experiences things.

31

In the highest state of *samadhi*, called Nirvikalpa Samadhi, the experience of the person that enters into that knowledge directly is mind-blowing and lasts for a long time; it is never forgotten and it also involves a real and effective change of state in the being. It is not like changing your mind about something or having a new idea of things. But there are relative degrees of the real, as according to the point of view of the creature self, whether dwelling at the causal or essential level. It is not that two contradictory things are true. One Brahma is true only but it is perceived differently according to the state of the being. For example, the one who is in the dreaming state thinks that world to be true but on waking up, he knows it to be false. To the being that knows his Self to be Brahma, both waking and dreaming states are relative or causal and so they are essentially non-existent for him. He knows as a fact that Brahma is the sole reality and all else an appearance. It does not need proving to him; he does not require proof anymore than he requires proof that he himself exists. The subject of discussion here is veritably the highest truth and knowledge, whether it is put in simple terms or more technically. According to the alchemists this also is said on the same subject:

> Every day men throw it away as dirt. Little children play with it in the streets.

What is this? It is the very subject of our discussion. The greater knowledge is simpler and yet also more profound than the lesser knowledge. The lesser degrees of knowledge are exceedingly complex as they deal with gross levels of manifestation. Conventional science, or modern material science, in spite of all its impressive products—everything from cell phones to atom bombs—is the very least of all knowledge. Consequently it is so complex that it requires specialists, each in their own field. This is to such an extent that the specialist in one field has no idea of what is known by the specialist in another field. Somewhere between those two extremes—metaphysical and material science—exists all the applications of traditional sciences. Ways of helping people enjoy a better and healthier, more trouble-free life, have been developed over thousands of years: there is Ayurvedic (natural) medicine, classical homeopathy and so forth. We do not teach or practice within those almost countless adaptations of knowledge for mundane purposes; our concern is the knowledge itself, which is the highest goal. Finally, question, objection, answer and refutation is a traditional method, and is proven to be effective. It is not the purpose of Advaita Vedanta though to merely give answers to questions or provide solutions to philosophical problems. It is the goal of Advaita to *dissolve* the question—and the questioner!

# The Four Great Statements: Mahavakyas

There are four Mahavakyas, or great statements on the nature of Reality, in the *Upanishads*.[17] All of them point to the fact that Brahma is consciousness and all that appears in the universe is no other than the light of this same consciousness. These great statements convey the essential teaching of the *Upanishads*, namely that Reality is one *sat-chit-ananda*, Brahma or pure being, consciousness and bliss. And that furthermore, the individual is essentially identical with Absolute Reality.

**1.** *Prajnanam Brahma*—Consciousness is Brahma

**2.** *Aham Brahmasmi*—I am Brahma

**3.** *Tat Tvam Asi*—That Thou Art

**4.** *Ayam Atma Brahma*—This Self is Brahma

Consciousness is Brahma: The statement provides a definition of Reality. Brahma, on the other hand, cannot be described—how can the Absolute be described? That would place a limit on the Absolute. All we can do is refer to it as *supra-essential essence*.[18] If we attach attributes then Brahma becomes 'qualified' as Brahma Saguna, and is then no different from Ishvara or the Lord of the Universe. Brahma is not a demiurge however; Brahma is consciousness Itself. We require instruments of hearing, feeling, seeing, tasting and smelling in order to perceive things, but without consciousness we could perceive nothing. It is only this consciousness that provides meaning to all of our experience. As it is written in the *shruti* texts, Brahma fills all space, is complete in Itself, and is continuously present in everything, from God down to the most minute particle of dust.[19] Brahma is one without a second; being everywhere, Brahma is also in each and every individual.

---

[17] These are commented on in *Panchadasi*, an Advaitan text consisting of fifteen chapters in three sections attributed to the sage Vidyaranya. The three sections are Viveka, *discrimination*, Dipa, *illumination* and Ananda, *bliss*—this last relating to *sat-chit-ananda*, being, consciousness and bliss that is no other than Brahma or the Supreme Identity.

[18] Translation of Swami Krishnananda.

[19] *Aitareya Upanishad.*

I Am Brahma: The 'I' is that which is the Witness, and stands apart from even the intellect. Contrary to what we imagine, it is also different from the ego-principle or I-sense, which merely borrows that light in order to perceive itself and other things, which it imagines to be entirely separate. That light of consciousness shines continuously through every act of thinking, feeling, seeing and so forth. The Witness (Atma), one without a second, is universal, and cannot be distinguished from Brahma, the Absolute. Hence the essential 'I' which is full, supra-rational and resplendent, is no different in reality from Brahma. We must carefully distinguish this from the identification of the individuality with Brahma. It is rather that Brahma, Absolute Reality, is the universal substratum of the individuality—and of all things that appear, and which we imagine to be reality. 'I am Brahma' does not point to an empirical relation between two entities; it rather affirms the non-duality of pure essence, as stated in the *Brihadaranyaka Upanishad*.

That Thou Art: This statement occurs in the *Chandogya Upanishad*. Sage Uddalaka mentions it nine times while instructing his disciple Svetaketu in the nature of Reality. *That* is Brahma or *sat-chit-ananda*, the one without a second, without name and form, and which always existed without birth or death. *That* Brahma finds an expression in Pure Being. Thou is 'you' but it does not refer to the ego or individuality as such. It is the innermost nature of the aspirant, which is wholly transcendent of intellect, mind, senses and reason. It is the real 'I'. The union of what seem to be two different things but that are not two things in reality is expressed by *Art*, or 'are'. We tend to think of supreme reality, the Real, as being something far away from us and completely separate, but this is a mistake, an error. The teaching, that it is really within us forever, is to destroy this ignorance. The true Self is not in any way subject to limitation or determination. It is one and the same as the Real, called Brahma. In some ways, this Tat Tvam Asi, 'That Thou Art', is the most important of the four great statements.

This Self is Brahma: The great statement occurs in the *Mandukya Upanishad*. What is referred to as *This* is the self-luminous and non-mediate nature of the Self, internal to everything and transcendent to it—whether it is the *ahankara* or individual ego or the physical body and the entire universe it seems to inhabit in its apparently separate existence. This Self is no other than Brahma, one without a second, which is the substratum of all things. That is to say, the real nature of all things is consciousness Itself. That which is everywhere is also within us, and what is within us is everywhere. It fills all space, expands into all existence or being, and is vast beyond all measure.

34

On account of self-luminosity, non-relativity and universality, Atma and Brahma are one and the same. It is important not to make the error of thinking that this involves an identification of the Self with the Absolute as though it were an act of bringing together two different things. The statement is there to teach that absoluteness or universality includes all things whatsoever, and that nothing at all can exist outside of it. This is the essence of the Advaitan realisation concerning the nature of Reality.

# Nirmala: I am Pure

Before we go more deeply into our subject, let us first consider something that frequently comes up whenever spirituality is discussed. The Greek word *agape* (αγαπη) does not translate directly in our language—we have only one word for love. Agape is translated somewhat narrowly in the New Testament as 'charity'; there are good reasons for this if we look into the etymology of that word, which has suffered a degraded meaning. Charity is related to *charis*, of which *charisma* shares a common root. Charity therefore includes love, kindness and grace—which are divine or spiritual attributes. However, a broader translation of *agape* is 'spiritual love'. It carries the implied sense of love and compassion that springs directly from knowing that God permeates all things.

This has been very greatly misunderstood in our times, a misunderstanding that owes to the degradation of our language and the incomprehension of anything spiritual. Emotional experience has thereby become a substitute for the spiritual, to the extent that it is now common for persons to think, and without even questioning it, that their emotional state has something to do with spirituality. Emotional experience or feeling is part of what it is to be human but it can have nothing to do with anything spiritual. Owing to this confusion of the spiritual with something completely ordinary we have the persistently populist fake notion of 'unconditional love', which is sometimes explained as a kind of 'pure emotion', and that is no less than an impossibility! How is this? The emotions cannot be purified because they are emotions—they are not pure by definition; they are emotive; they are plural, they are around for a while and then they change to something else. None of that is pure.

Unconditional love, by now a cliché, came out of New Psychology—which is by now quite old psychology. Some things have a way of becoming deeply entrenched in the collective mind-set especially when 'professionals' vigorously promote them. The New Psychology movement was influenced by Buddhism, but without knowledge of what that really is, within the context of its tradition, which is a very old one. New Psychology is characterised by its misappropriation of the spiritual by reductionism applied to the special language used to convey it in various traditions. Terms, often mistranslated in the first place, were torn out of the doctrines, taking them away from all spiritual context and discipline.

We can think about it: how can there be love without conditions? How can there be love unless there are at least two things? That is the condition, and in the human being all other conditions spring from that duality. However, the ultimate love is the love of God because God can lead us to direct knowledge, which *does* involve love without conditions because it is complete in itself. But anything else is conditional and certainly, in the sense that people use this notion of unconditional love, it does not transcend egoism and therefore attachment to objects—which is *all* the conditions!

One use of *agape* as an adverb conveys further subtle meaning to the word as used in spiritual context; it is no different from the once common English use, now archaic, of 'to be agape', implying that the mouth is wide open in wonder or astonishment. Here is the idea of emotional experience, common to all, but with connotations of the wonderment of spiritual insight or even realisation. The more ordinary uses of the verb include 'to receive with friendship', which is why the word is also given as 'brotherly love'. One special use of *agape* that is rare, and all the more interesting for that, was by early Christians, who celebrated a 'love feast', referring to a meal taken together in association with the Last Supper—so not a ceremonial Mass. The Eucharist formed part of this but it was not until a century or two later that it became distinct and separate from the love feast.[20]

Only Atma is pure. The Sanskrit word sometimes used as descriptive of Atma in Advaitan texts in this respect is Nirmala, 'I am Pure', but which literally is a negation, as Atma does not have qualities or attributes: 'I am not mixed'.[21] In truth, *agape* involves the full knowledge that the entire universe and all people and all creatures whatsoever, whether we happen to like or dislike them, are an expression of God and would not exist otherwise.

---

[20] This is reckoned to be somewhere between the end of the 1st century and midway through the 3rd century AD. From early on there are rumblings of disapproval from no less than St. Paul, 1 Corinthians 11: 17–34, who remarked on the lack of ceremony, to the extent of the informality being carried to gross behaviour such as not waiting for anyone else before eating and some getting drunk on wine! The love feast was gradually replaced with more austere procedures, such as fasting all day and then taking Communion in the evening. It is perhaps notable though that the tradition was continued in India and the Eastern Orthodox Church. In modern times anti-traditionalists including some Anglicans have revived the informal love feast, reducing it to something that is more or less indistinguishable from an open business lunch meeting.

[21] *Aparokshanubhuti* of Sri Shankaracharya 28: *Nirmalo nishcalo nantach.*

# What is the Real World?

We can now move on to considerations of the real and the unreal, from the point of view of Advaita Vedanta. That which we experience in our minds, through our sensory perceptions, is not *ultimately* real. That is not to deny that things exist at all. For example, if we were to have run out the door this morning without looking where we were going we would have fallen over the recycling boxes and bags in the driveway. Even if we had been in the state of Nirvikalpa, the highest *samadhi*, we would still have fallen over the recycling if we were not looking where we were going. So it would be foolish to deny that things exist as such in the relative or causal world. Advaita never denies experience, and on the contrary it uses everyday experience common to all to prove non-dual reality, step by step.

It is worth mentioning then that what we are studying here does not in any way contradict what are called the laws of physics, gravity and so forth. There are various forces that act together so that if we try and walk through a pile of boxes and bags we might fall over. Physics has a way of explaining this, in its own terms. Gravity is one such term, but in fact even scientists will usually admit they do not really understand what gravity even is. They can make theories about it based on observation and experiment. If we go to Quantum Physics then it is now admitted that consciousness, or at least thought, plays a part in the outcome of experiments upon which theories are based. If science were about truth there would be no need to keep inventing new theories to explain things. Later we will try and show by example how it is that even modern physics relies on indirect knowledge—that is knowledge gained by inference and yes, even faith, not direct Knowledge, which is the goal of Advaitan Yoga.

Viveka or discrimination is essential to Advaitan Self-Realisation. The primary difference to make is between the seer and the seen: if what we see is seen by ourselves, as the knower and experiencer of things, then there are two things, the seer and the seen. Obviously what is seen is then separate from ourselves and cannot be any part of Brahma, the real Self, the ultimate reality that is infinite and eternal, one without a second, with no parts, no separation, no beginning and no end. That, if you like, is the *claim* of Advaita Vedanta. No one is asked to believe this. We are asked to reflect upon it deeply in the light of our own experience first and foremost.

The knower, the seer of things, the experiencer, involves the mentality. The mind creates objects with the use of its sensory perceptions and faculties. If we think about it, we do not actually see things with our eyes. Putting it another way, our eyes do not see things. The eye is an instrument that receives impressions. These are conveyed through various nerves and so forth and simultaneously we 'see' an image in our mind. What we see is a mental image, formed from various impressions. This is not only direct cognition through 'seeing' but also involves memory, name and form. So the sensory impressions formed, or our knowledge of them, are formed from previous knowledge of other similar objects, and the previous knowledge of everyone else too, sometimes called 'conventional reality'. This is what can be called 'creations of the mind', because they are exactly that.

The sense of 'I' 'myself', the ego that thinks my mind and body is me, uniquely separate and different from all other creatures and things in the universe, is reflected light or consciousness—it is not the Consciousness, immortal, indestructible, that is called the Witness, or Atma or Purusha—there are many names for such things in Sanskrit. With that reflected light or consciousness in the 'small me', we use the faculties of mind and senses to think, to smell, taste, see, feel and hear things—five senses plus mind itself, the 'inward sense'. So it is that the I-sense is easily led to imagine that it is the mind and body, and it also becomes strongly attached to various external objects—though all are perceived internally.

The real Self, the Witness that is ever present, unchanging, is the source of that sentience that we use to know things, as we imagine. So although the Witness is not knowable as an object—because it is Consciousness Itself, not divided, not broken or separate in any way—we use it all the time! It is always there. It is only that we never usually think about it, let alone know it directly—which is another subject, as to how we can know something that is not knowable as an object. We will come on to this in a moment.

A word about terms: the use of capital letters in writing helps to distinguish the difference in the implied meaning, as we are using English translation of Sanskrit terms that do not have a direct translation in any modern language. So we have to carefully choose the terms we use and cannot use them in a conventional way. We have to invent a special use of our own language so as not to be mistaken.

39

A few special terms to be aware of are the Witness, the Seer, and the (supreme) Knower; these all refer to Atma, the infinite, undying, immortal Self. But similar terms such as seer, knower, without capitalisation, are used to describe the small self immersed in its cognitions and thinking them to be ultimate reality—even thinking them to be ourselves, or as belonging to us in some way. The body is the most powerfully persuasive possession. We think we are a body, or otherwise, if we are more spiritually advanced, we think we own a body and it belongs to us. Yet we are still mistaken and this can easily be proved: if we own a body and it belongs to us, then it is clearly a separate thing, apart from us, me, you, 'I'. If it is separate then how can it be that undivided 'one' that is the Self, the Witness of all that has no parts, Atma? The truth is, and which can hardly be denied, we experience the body as an object. Is that not so? If we experience it as an object then it is apart from our Self in reality. I am not my body. Once we see the difference between pure consciousness and mind, we can also say 'I am not my mind'.

The Witness, Atma-consciousness, makes our seeing and knowing of objects possible. Or to put it another way—and to be really exact because Atma does not 'make' anything, does not act or participate in sensory appearances—Atma is that which *appears to be the cause* in the relative world, from the corporeal point of view. However, if we take it another step, and realise the world of appearances, cause and effect, as an illusion like the rope mistaken for a snake in a dark room, then there is only the cause, the rope. And because there is no effect, there is no cause either. Thus in reality Atma is without cause and does not cause anything. Atma alone *is*. All else is an appearance.

In the texts of Advaita, the world of appearances is called 'false'— that is the word that is used. It is interesting to note that some modern Hindu sages, when addressing Western, English-speaking people, have taken to use the term 'transactional reality' to describe the world of appearances, even though they will continue to assert it is really false. The reason given is that modern minds feel very uncomfortable with having 'their reality' described as false. In fact, they get very aggressive when defending what Advaita calls their ignorance! So some use the term *transactional reality* so they do not have to put up with the snapping, snarling dogs of reason that are so easily provoked.

The mind creates an entire world in dreams. This leads on to the thought that even the whole world, as we perceive it, is a creation of mind. This is one area where we need to be very careful with words so note the way in which this was put, *as we perceive it*. The notion of objectivity then becomes less certain than it is in the usual case, when we do not even think about it. That is also true of all discursive thought, which depends on language that is in itself symbolic. The question of objective reality is well accounted for in the scriptures and commentaries going back to very ancient times. It is all held within the doctrine, and so we will expound on this a little. There are two exact terms in Sanskrit that can be very useful here, because there are no words in our language for such things:

**1.** Maha-aksha—the great (world) appearance.

**2.** Chitta-aksha—the small (i.e. personal world) appearance.

Maha-aksha: When our bodies die and we depart the corporeal domain we can be reasonably well assured that the great world appearance will continue for all other people and creatures on this earth. Not forever, but for perhaps a long time. Also we should be aware that 'on this earth' relates to a tiny fraction of all possible worlds but there is no space here to go into all that. So that Maha-aksha, literally 'great object of seeing', is that appearance said to be caused by Maya in the Hindu doctrines.

Chitta-aksha: When we go to sleep at night, as well as when our physical bodies die, the personal world-reality dissolves and we imagine it, or other worlds, in dream—or it dissolves altogether with our minds in the deep dreamless sleep. As soon as we awaken from sleep, that world reappears. We remember the appointment we have later in the day. We recollect the embarrassing thing we said the day before, or the annoying person that deliberately provoked us. We remember who we are, by name, where we were born, our 'history', all the rest of the 'me identifications'. But all those can disappear even in sleep as if they never existed. And yet even in deep sleep the Witness sees that blankness of having no mind. Imagine this: in deep sleep we know nothing of it and remember nothing of it. The mind is not there, it is not thinking or dreaming. We are totally unaware of our body in that state. And yet the Witness, Atma, is always and forever there.

So suppose it were possible to be in that deep sleep and yet be completely wide-awake at the same time? Then we would see Atma rising like a thousand suns in the sky simultaneously. That it is how it is put poetically in the Vedanta though it is no exaggeration either. Not only that but it is also even possible sometimes, though it is very rare it seems. It is in the very word, 'object-ive', that we see we are speaking of an object or objects perceived as outside of ourselves. This objective world is undoubtedly composed of objects in the mind, of that there can be no doubt at all. Do these objects exist 'out there'? Certainly; but we also experience 'out there' in our minds, through our sense perceptions.

Could we not then say that Maya *is* the mind-created world? Advaita puts it exactly the other way round: the mind-created world is possible through the covering or veiling power of Maya. We do not create any world out of our own personal power. That power belongs to Maya, and in fact Maya and Brahma (or God) are not two separate things. Maya is the power of God to cover things and to project an appearance—it is a dual power. But we can look at it both ways. We can go even further than that and say that the mind itself is the product of Maya. No Maya, no mind! Pure consciousness *is* and always is.[22]

From all this arises a further question: How then can we trust our insights and knowing? The question comes from the side of the knower, the experiencer and doer of things. Firstly, it is always put forward in spiritual practice that one should trust in God and Guru first and foremost. In the modern secular world we are encouraged to trust in ourselves, even when we know we are ignorant! In the postmodern world this is pushed so far as to become 'truth is what you make of it'. Anything else is then written off as absolutism.

As an aside, because it is not central to this discussion: the post-industrial world of politics and business is now governed by 'truth is relative', 'truth is what you make of it', and once this is known—it is well known in academia but not in the public domain—the bizarre, chaotic nature of certain world events and governance becomes simple to understand.

---

[22] There is a further distinction to be made over the use of terms. Maya, with a capital letter, refers to the supreme Shakti power of the universe, while *maya*, without a capital letter, is the effect or appearance itself, called ignorance.

There is a postmodern philosophy behind it that can be learned and taught. They know it at the UCLA and Berkeley, Harvard, Oxford and Cambridge, in economics and business studies, but it is over the heads of the general public who are nonetheless ready and eager to accept the latest popularised theories of neuroscience that want to persuade them into thinking that consciousness is generated from insentient matter. They are ready to believe, if they do not believe it already, that they are really only neuro-biological machines. That is a digression but we think it is quite an interesting one.

The word *faith* is better than trust, while we are talking about the spiritual, because trust is an ordinary thing. A business that sells products wants us to trust in the business and their products so sales and profits increase. Faith is misunderstood in our world today, because it is mistaken for 'belief', in the way of thinking something is true simply because we want to believe it. There is no trace of such a notion in Advaita Vedanta. The real meaning of *faith* includes a certain element of knowledge, and that is where we start to answer the question. Insights and knowing are always a matter of the mind but we need them all the same, just as we need our minds and reason. If we go back to trust, the word originally used, it is curious to think how much we trust our own insights and knowing all the time. How else do we even leave the house to cross the road? More than that, we are ready to trust in other people and even machines constantly. If you drive a car you trust it is not going to break down in some remote place, although that can happen sometimes. But that possibility will not mean you keep your car in the garage at all times. If we want to fly by an airline to another state or country, we trust that the pilot will fly us there and that the engines will not drop off the plane at 40,000 feet. Is it not astonishing then to see how trust disintegrates as soon as it comes to anything of a spiritual nature?

The caveat there, when it comes to trust, mind and reason is that even in the regular or ordinary case we easily let our minds and reason go to places that are mindless and unreasonable. We do it far more than anyone cares to admit. And then we even allow ourselves to be guided by that. This also takes place on a mass or collective scale. It is like being shown the way out of a madhouse by one of the lunatics in residence. How do we know the madman is not showing us the way into a cell we can never escape from? In fact, though it might be unbelievable to some, that is also descriptive of university education.

From the Advaitan point of view, while we might need a diploma or degree for something or the other, it is nonetheless all ignorance and not real knowledge. It is only 'knowledge of the mind' (*chitta-jnana*).

Advaita Vedanta is very clear but confusions arise because it is our own minds that want to play tricks on us—because the mind does not want us to know reality. At least, not until we train the mind to go in another direction than the one it has learned by habit, which is all to reinforce the ego sense of separation. The mind has been king of the king's palace for a long time, and now we are saying, 'You are not the king!' This is shocking. It is like saying to the President, 'You are not the President!' That is not going to be much liked by him and he will gather his army of statesmen and politicians to defend the case. He even has the military if he is really pushed to it and can bomb us all out of existence. Faced with that, we are usually ready to believe what he wants us to believe.

So let us return to faith, which when understood correctly includes a certain element of knowledge. Actually, it can be very surprising how much faith is involved in completely ordinary things. Religion and science are not as different as people like to imagine. In fact, they are like two peas in a pod. If we see a star rising at night very clearly with our own eyes, how do we know it is actually a gigantic ball of thermo-nuclear reactions a million times bigger than the earth—which we cannot see with our own eyes in entirety? We only know that because we believe what we learned in science books. We cannot touch that star. We cannot walk around it. We cannot feel it, smell it, taste it or hear it. We *see* it in our minds.

How do we know for sure what it really is? We see a point of light, twinkling and somewhat beautiful to our minds—it conveys a 'sense of eternity'. We are not saying here that we disagree with science that the star is a great mass of thermo-nuclear reactions. We might also say that while we can agree with that, it is a strictly limited way of understanding things. It works in its own way, yes, but it does not really take us very far in knowledge of reality.

Faith that there is something of truth in Advaita includes an element of non-ordinary knowledge. In fact even without faith, even thinking 'there might be something in it', presupposes some innate knowing beyond the level of ordinary knowledge—which includes all of conventional sciences. As we have previously mentioned, the Advaitan explanation for objective reality as well as dream reality is *maya*, which is also called ignorance in the same way that when we awaken from a dream, we know it was a dream and not real.

44

Otherwise it is like believing in the movie and not knowing that there are actors pretending to be characters, and that have learned a script, that have been filmed, and the film is an illusion projected on a screen. Ignorance is to believe in the movie as total reality and having no idea of the projection, the screen, and the audience watching it. Or that the movie will come to an end and then a new one begins. Maya is not only the movie, the screen and the audience but is also *the space that the entire show takes place in*. And behind all that, the substratum is Brahma, or God Absolute.

There is ever a doubt in the mind of the one that struggles to understand anything truly existing beyond our own minds and bodies and a multiplicity of exterior objects. Maya cannot be understood from within *maya*. This is not something we can know from figuring it out. It is not a mind-puzzle, to be worked out or known only by highly specialised professors or logicians. We can give you, if you are one that doubts all this, something substantial to be going on with. We can take Brahma as a paradigm here because we are discussing Advaita Vedanta: Brahma Nirguna is the Supreme Absolute. This cannot be known by the mind, by working it out, by arguing or reasoning. Otherwise, we would all be Moses, Ramakrishna, Jesus Christ, Buddha and so forth, would we not? Actually, there is an Advaitan secret here: we *are* all those luminaries, but in our real Self, not our ego. If Brahma did not exist then we and nothing else could exist. Take everything away and Brahma remains. That is what we truly are, if only we can know it and see it as clearly as we see the world of objective things.

# How Can We Know God?

How can the mind know Brahma when we are told the mind cannot know Brahma? The *Upanishads* tell us both things in different places: that we can know Brahma and that we cannot know Brahma. Hold on to this one because it is really important: there is the Sanskrit term, *Brahma Vritti*, 'the thought of Brahma'. This is the one thought that leads to identification with the Witness or Atma that is one with Brahma. To do this as a practice to an advanced level, other thoughts than Brahma really need to be shut out from the mind. But even a little of Brahma can take us a long way. When that thought is held to, *Brahma reveals Itself*.

Another useful Sanskrit word for what we are discussing here is *Brahmadhyasa*. This is meditating, reflecting or conversing on Brahma, or studying of the Vedas—but always aimed at direct knowledge. It is not a scholarly pursuit. That direct knowledge, not known by the mind, is *Brahma Jnana*, which indicates the highest knowledge. It is also *aparokshanubhuti*, literally 'direct realisation (of Brahma), not reflected or indirect knowledge'. That is the goal. All else must lead towards that.

It is true, having reached even this stage in understanding that we can feel we are beginning to lose our hold on things! Advaita is Non-dualism so it does not admit to two things existing. There cannot be a 'Real' and a thing called objective reality, as if two separate things exist. The analogy used again and again is that of the rope and the snake: the rope symbolises Brahma and the snake symbolises *maya*, the appearance of things. When we know the snake is really a phantom and what we are seeing is a rope, we no longer see the snake. It is likewise with a mirage in the desert. The mirage looks like it is really water but when we walk over there we see that it is a trick of the senses that makes it appear as though there was real water. The desert sand and the mirage of flowing water are not two things. Only the desert sand is real, in this example.

In the case of Maya, the power that causes the greater objective world appearance, it helps to remember that Maya is the Shakti power of God no less. What a powerful illusion that is! And yet, that same power is the power that can lead us to knowing God or Brahma, through knowledge. Knowledge and Mind, as well as small mind, also belong to Maya, and there is the key to it all. That is why it is said that true Knowledge is by the grace of God, or is a gift of God. Knowing the truth in that is also the gift of God to know it.

This directly leads on to the consideration of the verbal practice of saying (or thinking), 'I am not this body; I am not this mind'. For sure, saying it without direct knowledge is an act of faith but even the smallest act of faith can bring the most undreamed of rewards. Advaita Vedanta insists that only knowledge destroys ignorance *and we need our minds for that*. This can be explained; otherwise it begins to look as though the goal is to be mindless!

The mind is not self-luminous. Here is another useful analogy: imagine the sun, the visible sun, but as a symbol of Brahma. Then the mind is like a polished metal plate, or a mirror. If the sunlight strikes that mirror or reflecting surface, and we happen to be standing in an otherwise dark room, we can point the mirror at objects in the room and they will be made luminous so we can see them. Move the mirror somewhere else, and in the same way as if we were holding a torch, the objects will disappear and something else will be made luminous. But the mirror does not illuminate things with its own light; it is reflecting the light of the sun.

Taking this one step further, and using the analogy of a torch: does the light from the torch really illuminate objects? Think on this: you see that light in your mind, using your eyes as the physical instrument and your sense of sight as receptor. The torch does not know or see anything. The torch produces the physical light but you see the illumination in the light of the mind, which is reflected light.[23]

The mind is needed before knowledge can destroy ignorance. There are three kinds of knowledge: cognitive knowledge of perception, knowledge of inference, and the direct knowledge or realisation of the Supreme Identity, Brahma. But all destroy ignorance in their own way. For example, supposing we are ignorant of European history in the thirteenth century? We need to read some books or go to some lectures or classes, and that ignorance is destroyed.

---

[23] Here is a curious fact: if we look at a dollar bill on the reverse side, there is an eye in a triangle in a blaze of glory over a truncated pyramid. There is one eye there, not two. The triangle is an ancient symbol for what is seen, what appears, but is in reality one. There is an entire numerical symbolism behind it too: $\sum (1-2) = 3$ and so forth ad infinitum. In the Bible and in Freemasonry the capstone on the top is 'the stone the builders rejected' because the builders did not know what it was. In Christianity, Christ is that capstone.

In the same way, but on the level of direct realisation, Paul the Roman, who persecuted early Christians, saw God on the road to Damascus and his ignorance of God was destroyed. He went on to become one of the greatest saints and teachers of Christianity. So there is no paradox here: knowledge destroys ignorance. If we do not have knowledge then no matter what else we do or think we are still ignorant.

We have also said sometimes that we are what we *know*—and not what we think or do or see: this is worthy of contemplation and even the deepest meditation. Why is this? It is because nothing in the world is apart from Brahma or God. God, as the expression of the Absolute, is Pure Being. What is Pure Being? It is pure Consciousness. It is not knowledge in the sense of a knower and a thing that is known. It is Knowledge Itself. The world—whether we see it or not—is the product of Maya, without beginning or end. Maya cannot be explained from within *maya*, the appearance that is otherwise called the great world illusion. Shaktimaya has two powers: the projecting of Brahma as an appearance and the covering or hiding of the Real. These two powers are really one and the same. Maya does this through Name and Form (*nama* and *rupa*). All things are only able to appear through the power of Name and Form.

The Adam that gave names to things in the Bible was not actually a man of flesh and blood; the name there was used to mean Pure Being or Universal Man (as known to the Arabs). In Sanskrit, it is Hiranyagarbha. To the ancient Persians, it was Mithras. So Adam in that context is the Logos, no less than God or Ishvara the Lord of the Universe as it is called in Sanskrit. In all this there are deep mysteries. This concerns the relation between man, God and the universe no less. And some of that is of a truly esoteric nature, that is to say, very rarely written about or discussed. Why not written? This is because the very nature of revelation, in the true and special sense of that, is only conveyed through symbolism. Words and letters are symbols, but they are secondary. One might then think that if we study hieroglyphics we might get direct knowledge but that is not so ipso facto. One must have knowledge before such things may be construed without error.

All the same, it is an essential part of doctrine in all traditions that by reading the sacred scriptures, called *shruti* or 'direct' texts in Hinduism, it is possible to know God or even Brahma Absolute. They go further than that. While merely reading a book will not convey such knowledge, the same cannot be gained without study and deep immersion of the whole self in such texts.

Meditation practice is needed. In all traditions the guru cannot be dispensed with, however much that rails against the prejudice of the modern mentality. The one that says 'We cannot know', the agnostic, only makes a declaration of his own ignorance, as does the atheist, who says that 'God does not exist'—and in so doing, denies his own existence.

# Tiger of Fear

Why do people become fearful when the truth is put to them? We know they do because in questions at lectures or classes, or in letters or other writings, they sometimes express anger and frustration. Fear does not arise from knowledge; fear arises from unknowing or ignorance of truth. We will cling on with both hands to something even when it is being pointed out very clearly that it is nothing but an illusion. It is like seeing a fearsome tiger in a forest. In fright, we climb a tree to escape. If we were to look closer we would see that the great head is nothing but a tree stump and the stripes are merely sunlight and shadows playing on the ground. Once we know this we can walk right up to the tiger and see it is nothing but an illusion, a trick of light and shadow. We no longer have to run away from the tiger because we know there is no tiger at all. If we do not know this, then we must continue to take action to escape the jaws of the frightful beast.

Advaitan texts seek to loosen this grip, this clinging to illusion, bit by bit, until what remains is the truth. Of all the things that cause consternation among those who are interested in Non-dualism but have not yet gained a foothold on knowledge that is in any way stronger than what has been gained through 'ordinary life', as René Guénon termed it, *maya* or the world appearance comes top of the list—it might be an illusionary tiger but it is a very fascinating one! It is worth paraphrasing Guénon first, so we can understand what is meant by 'ordinary life':[24]

Modern man has become quite impermeable to any influences other than such as impinge on his senses; not only have his faculties of comprehension become more and more limited, but also the field of his perception has become correspondingly restricted. From this severe limitation arises the notion of 'ordinary life' or 'everyday life'. This is a life in which nothing that is not purely human can intervene in any way, owing to the elimination from it of any sacred, ritual, or symbolical character. Everything that surpasses conceptions of that order is, even when it has not yet been expressly denied, at least relegated to the domain of the extraordinary, and is regarded as exceptional, strange, and unaccustomed. This is a reversal of the normal order as represented by integrally traditional civilisations where the possibility of spiritual influence goes without question.

---

[24] René Guénon, *The Reign of Quantity and the Signs of the Times*, Chapter Fifteen [Sophia Perennis].

The abnormality of the modern mentality is such that the profane conception is even called 'real life'. In the modern world, as soon as we are born we are subjected to this anti-spiritual notion and it is heavily reinforced in every conceivable way until the spiritual, as something ultimately real, not an abstract conception, or something to do with human feelings and emotions, is so far removed as to be invisible.

We must be careful in the language we use. If we use terms borrowed from 'ordinary life', the world of those without knowledge, we place ourselves at risk of partaking in the same ignorance. When we deal with profane or worldly people we can use the same language they use but we need to use special terms to speak or write about the knowledge gained from *viveka*. What often happens is that a student, confronted suddenly with a host of unfamiliar terms, tries to find clarity by comparing what they read or hear with what they have already assimilated from their environment or from what they have learned elsewhere. In regard to spiritual matters, 'ordinary life' is always wrong because it is a kind of mentality that excludes all real spiritual possibilities and that creates fake substitutions.

We will provide some further examples later, but firstly let us consider the 'problem'—for some students will want to see it like that—of Maya. In fact, the real problem as such is that the student is fascinated by the examples given, various forms of illusion such as a rope mistaken for a snake, but cannot look to where the example is pointing, which is to the true Self, Atma, which is metaphysical. As Atma is not perceptible by the senses, which borrow the light of Atma consciousness, so it is that many persons, instead of making the much greater effort needed to meditate on what is being pointed at, the Real, will raise endless questions about Maya and her mysterious power to delude men. All they are doing is staying with the delusion. All the same, we will patiently explain what needs to be explained.

Quite often then, it will seem as if Maya and the Real (Atma or Brahma) are two entirely separate things, and there must exist a kind of opposition between them. This is false as there are not two things. Sri Shankaracharya devoted a small book to this subject, entitled 'Enquiry into the Nature of the Seer and the Seen'.[25] It is important to be clear as to what we mean when we say 'seer' as that can mean either the individual, that thinks he is the knower and the doer of things, or the Witness called Atma, that does not participate in the seeming world of cause and effect.

---

[25] *Drg Drsya Viveka.*

51

In the case of the Witness, then Seer is usually spelled with a capital letter. We must firmly establish that Maya is not part of 'things as they are'; Maya is that power that produces things as they *seem to be*. There is no relationship of 'creation' with regard to the Seer, Atma or the Witness—otherwise called the Real. So far as the individual 'seer' goes, he also does not create anything that is not already his Self unless we consider that an illusion can be created from the mind going to work on the sensory impressions. Otherwise, how can an unreal thing be created? We can take the Advaitan example of the sun reflected in the water of a lake. We can see a perfectly clear image of the sun in the water, especially if the water is completely calm and still. Does the sun create that image as a separate thing from itself? Clearly it is not the case. If we take away the sun the image disappears. It is nothing but the illusion made by the play of light on the surface of the water. So we cannot say there is a relation of 'creation' between the sun and its reflected image. This same analogy is used to explain the *jiva*, the individual self, which is a reflection of Atma, the true Self. The individual person does not really create the world; he (as the ego) is not a demiurgic God. What he sees is a covering or veil of ignorance, the unknowing of the Real.

Maya cannot be understood from within *maya*. This is because Maya has two powers: projection, the positive side of it, and covering or veiling, which is the negative side of it—though these two powers are really one. So the question sometimes arises, 'Are we not always within *maya*?' This assumes that 'we', or 'I myself', are always in a state of ignorance or delusion. If that were true then obviously faith in any body of teaching or teacher would be mistaken, because no one could know anything about the Real. And if there were any teaching in that world then it would certainly be a case of the 'blind leading the blind'! An enlightened person is one who is not deluded by Maya. The universe continues to appear as it always does but he is not fooled by any of it. In a state of *samadhi*, the yogin sees only God everywhere.

The five kinds of cognitions as named in Ashtanga Yoga also cause some confusion. In the *Yoga-Sutras* there are listed five kinds of *pramanas*. The first is direct or valid cognition of a real thing, be it cat, pot, tree, bird, etc. The second is cognition gained by language or words alone (*vikalpa*). A word is not a real thing as such but we need it to communicate. Then there is totally false cognition, as with the Advaitan example of the 'horns of a hare' (*viparyaya*). Then there is cognition from something remembered (*smrti*). Lastly there is lack of cognition, amounting to absence or a blank state (*nidrā*).

It has been put to us that if a child sees a bird for the first time and someone explains to them what a bird is, that is the last time that the child sees a bird for what it is. This is false, and no doubt there is a trace of sentimentality in the way it is put, which betrays it. Firstly, this rests on an erroneous assumption that if a child sees something for the first time that must be a direct cognition as it does not rest on inference. It may be that it is a direct cognition but it is still produced in the same way that any of us will see something—it is formed from sensory perception. It is smelled, tasted, seen, felt or heard, or a combination of those things. Once we are told that it has a name, 'bird', for example, we can attach name and form to what we perceive. So some of what we are talking about here is a matter of experience, or lack of experience. One may meditate on the same bird and realise the nature of that animal with a depth of profundity that eclipses the childish wonder at seeing the bird for the first time. A child does not have any grasp on the Real that is the subject of our enquiry. Lack of experience does not equal knowledge, whether it is ordinary knowledge or special knowledge.

The direct cognition *pramaña* involves a perceptible form; in the case of our bird example, it is something that is seen. In all ancient traditions, not only the Hindu, name (*nama*) comes before form (*rupa*). According to St. John the Evangelist, 'In the beginning was the word [Logos], and the word was with God'. So in the case of a child seeing a bird for the first time, what came first, the form or the name? The child does not know it is a bird until someone says so. In other languages it will be something else—many languages follow the Sanskrit root *ava*, *avian* and so forth, indicative of something with wings, that flies through the air. Once the child is told the name, it is prone to utter that word often until it is learned, at first imperfectly: 'bud, bud...' This impulse to articulate, to match a verbalism with things perceived is deeply ingrained in us, and it is latent within the child. How then is it that the name, the *nama*, comes before the form, the *rupa*? The word for a thing, which becomes simultaneous in the mind with that very thing, is only the grossest manifestation of name, *nama*. The name, at its root, is much subtler than that. It is the real 'essence' of that creature, person or thing, the 'root vibration' we might say, that distinguishes it from other things. Therefore, 'In the beginning was the word'. We should note also that name and form are two powers belonging to Maya, the cosmic Shakti or soul of the world, and of God.

Inference by name and form on the gross level is essential while we are dealing with the world of relative cause and effect. The mistake is to think that any of that is the 'real world'. The purpose of *viveka* discrimination is to constantly remind us that the appearance of a universe full of separate things, as perceived by a mind and body, which we imagine to be Self, is false, an error. The mind experiences a world of things and creatures through the sensory impressions received by the mind. But what experiences the mind? That is the nature of our enquiry here. Advaita is not concerned with what we experience or how we experience it, cognitions, dreams and the like. Advaita is concerned with the experiencer, and the nature of who we really are. We are not what we smell, taste, see, touch and hear—this has been established. In that way, there is no real difference between what is an internal perception and what is an external perception, because we only experience things as external to ourselves out of the ignorance of thinking we are a separate light in the universe that does not owe to any source other than mind and body.

Here is another example of the importance of being precise with language: There is often talk of 'spiritual growth' in the popular domain, but what is spiritual does not increase or decrease. What is really meant is spiritual 'development' but even that is wrong. The spiritual does not change and is not subject to time and space, birth or death. We are really talking about the individual developing so that any spiritual realisation might be possible. But when people will speak about 'spiritual growth' they use those terms because they have no idea of what spirituality really is. They think it is something to do with body and mind and they cannot see anything that transcends that.

When understood in its proper sense, such development in all traditions includes the strengthening of faith, which is derived from strength in itself. Faith in guru and God, considered essential in all traditions, nonetheless arouses consternation in the modern mind. In faith, a certain germ of knowledge is implicit, and it is from there that faith is 'strengthened' until there is real conviction of the truth. This conviction does not arise from belief or being persuaded by a powerful argument; it arises from experience and knowledge, which acts as a support to direct realisation. With direct realisation, faith is no longer needed. Do we need proof that the sun shines? Do we need faith to know that? No. We can see that the sun shines. So it is with Atma, that is no different from Brahma, one without a second.

Non-dualism, which is the literal meaning of Advaita, causes confusion in itself, even once it is accepted. For example the question arises: Can the dualistic world of reason and words be used as a contemplative proof of Non-dual reality? Certainly it can but we have to be aware that such reality, the sole Real, cannot be proved as if it was some ordinary thing. It is not an object but proof would involve other objects—there would be no end to it. Again we would put the question, 'Do you need proof that you exist?' On the other hand, all the works of Sri Shankaracharya, for example, set out to show that Non-dualism can indeed be understood by reason and experience. Advaita Vedanta is a wholly rational science, even if it points to something entirely transcendent of the reason and mind. We need to be clear about the difference between reasoning and *dualism*, which is a philosophical school of thought (*darshana*). Dualism rests on the assumption that the universe involves multiple 'real' things. Advaita, 'Not two', insists that supreme reality is not in any way divided otherwise it would be limited, reduced and qualified. There is a difference to be discerned between reasoning about Non-dual reality and 'dualism'. Dualism rests on a belief in universal multiplicity and nothing that transcends that divided state.

Finally, if there are not two things (in reality) then where does love, or more specifically Agape, spiritual love, come into it? As we said before, in truth, *agape* involves the full knowledge that the entire universe and all people and all creatures whatsoever, whether we happen to like or dislike them, are an expression of God and would not exist otherwise.[26] Love, when seen in that way makes sense and meaning out of everything. Sages that enter into direct experience of the Real do not encounter a loveless reality. It might even be said that love and the Real are inseparable and, essentially, are 'not two things'!

While it is sometimes seen that Advaita is the crown of it all and Karma and Bhakti Yoga lower degrees, it can also be seen as the basis of it all, the substratum of the Real, called Brahma. The supreme realisation does not imply giving up the practice, including devotion to God or otherwise devotion to helping others in that light. Advaita very much encourages Karma and Bhakti Yoga, and not in any way as a means to an end—which would be the error of doing ritual only in the hope of getting some reward, for example. It is more the case that love, devotion and service are greatly purified and strengthened through knowledge of the Real.

---

[26] See 'Nirmala: I am Pure'.

# What is Death to the Soul?

Questions concerning the soul, and what happens to it after physical death, are made difficult by the word 'soul' itself. In English we have only the one word, soul, which can mean a variety of different things. So unless we know what we mean when we use that word we are cast adrift. In Hinduism, the word soul is often taken as Self (with a capital) in which case it means Atma. But as the individuality, which is closer to what it means in English, it is more *jivatma* or *ahankara*. In general or conventional usage, the English word soul only means the mentality, even feelings and emotions or the psychological component, and that is no use to us at all. It is best then if we look at the soul in terms of the Hindu doctrine, otherwise it can be anything you like. There is also a treatise on the soul that we have written, using very specialised terminology but it includes Sanskrit terms so as to be precise. In that book, the soul is called the Scarlet Woman, and she is referred to the elemental nature.[27] This includes the three envelopes of being on the subtle form level:[28]

**1.** The Intellectual (*boddhi*; inclusive of *anhankara*).

**2.** The Mentality (*manas*; thought and mental faculties).

**3.** Action and Sensation (*pranas* and senses).

It is reasonable to simplify all this down to the 'elemental nature', however imperfect that is. The 'woman of blood', another term used for the soul or Scarlet Woman, includes everything we normally think of as 'life', 'me', 'my existence', as typically identified with body and mind. The journey of the Scarlet Woman is to get initiated and realise she is infinitely greater than that. The terminology is simple but fits with our actual experience.

The soul fears death greatly because she is identified with body and mind and the body at least will surely die and become nothing but a pile of ashes. The soul has also identified her mind very closely with her body so as not to realise they are completely as separate as you are from your writing pad.

---

[27] *Law of Thelema—Hidden Alchemy.*

[28] For a detailed explanation see *Metamorphosis—Hermetic Science and Yoga Power.*

As soon as we are born into physical existence the one absolutely certain thing is we—meaning our bodies—will die. It is written into the contract so to speak and there is nothing we can do to get out of it. The question is, *what is it that dies?* It is certainly not Atma, which is deathless, immutable and so forth.

From the Advaitan point of view, being born into another life is only another round of experiencing temporary pleasure and pain, growing old, sickness and death—over and over again, until we are sick of it and want to become enlightened and find freedom from all that forever. So Advaita does not concern itself all that much with the details of all that happens after death and questions arising therefrom but it accepts the general doctrine as a basis: it is the subtle part, not the gross part, that is able to transmigrate.

The doctrine of transmigration, which bears no resemblance to modern 'reincarnationism', is embedded in Hinduism, Jainism and Buddhism; it is in the Egyptian tradition and seems to have been in the Orphic and other ancient initiatic traditions.[29] This is why secular funerals, very popular in our country now, which involve no religious part whatsoever and only remember the person's life are a total disaster in spiritual terms. People think they are only body and mind so when death comes that is it—like switching off a television set. Some of the subtle anatomy can linger for some time after physical death and a main part of religious rites is to cut that short and give the soul a chance to know God and get a better birth in another life or otherwise attain salvation or liberation, however that is understood. In that case there is a kind of translation of the soul, an upward transposition to higher states, which is helped by rites such as in Christianity properly understood.

According to the doctrine of the transmigration of the soul, death and birth are indefinite in so far as we are unable to put a number on how many there might be. We cannot say, 'We will have ten thousand births and deaths and then no more'. It is not measurable by quantity but at the same time, the births and deaths are *not infinite*. We can transmigrate to higher worlds, for example the celestial worlds, populated by *devas* and *devis*, we can even become such gods—and may have been in former lives. But an end comes to all such existences eventually unless we fully realise we are Parambrahma, the infinite, absolute, eternal, *sat-chit-ananda*.

---

[29] See 'Reincarnationism', *Metamorphosis* [ibid].

The Jiva can form a new body and mind—in fact it is really *jivatma* that does this.[30] If we are religious we will say it is God that determines it. We do not remember anything about former existences; when the reincarnationists think they can do that they are deluding themselves totally. Advanced yogins can use Samyama Yoga to know something about it, or they could once, but that is very exceptional.[31]

It needs to be understood, to avoid confusions, that the human state is not the ultimate of any series of births—because sequential time is only a determination of the human state. Admittedly, this can become quite complex, which is one reason perhaps why it is not written or spoken about much. There is general agreement though that the human state, which only comes about once, as do all other states, has a unique opportunity to know God, or Atma and Brahma as one, and to obtain liberation (*moksha*).

The *boddhi* or higher intellect is the principle of the individuality in man. It is sometimes likened to a ray from the sun, where the sun symbolises Atma. One might then ask, does that 'ray' of which the reflection is *jivatma* continue after physical death? It is the physical body, first and foremost, that dies with the physical death. The subtle body, as previously stated, can continue to a certain extent, and which allows transmigration.

However, from the strictly Advaitan point of view, we can counter such a question with this: does a ray of the sun continue after the sun goes down in the evening? No. And yet the sun is still there. We must remember that a ray is not a physical or real object either, it is an analogy. We can see the sun reflected on a surface and so we say the image is caused by a ray of the sun—but the ray is not actually a 'thing'. We cannot catch a ray of the sun and keep it in a jar. The sun's light is not divided into parts and so it is for Atma—Atma is not divisible into parts.

---

[30] Once the Supreme Realisation is gained, then it is also realised that the Jiva and Atma are not two things. One must think of the rope and snake analogy: there are not two things, rope and snake. Only the rope is the real (Brahma). The snake is an appearance brought about by the dual projection and covering power of Maya.

[31] See *Metamorphosis*, where the Supernormal Powers are explained in great detail.

The *boddhi* forms the individuality; the individuality does not emerge from the mind or body. It is sometimes said by Egyptologists and others that the ancient Egyptians must have believed the latter, but this rests on a misunderstanding of symbolism.[32] The *boddhi* is the instrument by which Atma knows individual mind and body. It is also that by which knowledge can be gained of other states of being such as are found in the celestial worlds, including gods or *devas*. If a new individual mind and body is formed, as in the doctrine of transmigration, then a *boddhi* principle must exist as it is the root of that individuality but to all intents and purposes it cannot be said to be the same *boddhi* that formed a previous one. It has dissolved into the *prakriti* 'substance', involving the three Gunas, and has then emerged again so it is in no way a replica of what it was; and what it was and what it is, is in any case a relative existence, not an absolute one.

Now arises a further important question regarding the soul, which as has already been stated can transmigrate. How can it be then that the soul can pass through many states on the way to the goal of realisation and yet it is often implied that the soul can perish? This kind of question can carry some erroneous presumptions. For example, some will readily assume that there is a sort of 'purpose' to transmigration, which is very dangerously close to the Theosophical notion of a succession of human lives likened to 'lessons' where we 'evolve'. There is nothing at all like that in traditional doctrine or in Advaitan source texts. The superimposition or covering upon the Real called *maya* is without beginning or end until knowledge destroys ignorance and we are free forever. That is the Non-dual view. Our writings and the scriptures of various ancient traditions nonetheless accept the dreadful possibilities of:

**1.** Hell and great suffering and torment to the soul in the postmortem state(s) as well as in earthly existence.

**2.** Total annihilation of the soul.

In Hinduism, the first possibility is seldom mentioned. However, it is an essential part of the doctrine—if there are higher worlds then there are lower worlds too, including the worlds of demons or *asuras*, and a region where no light can enter at all. Hinduism therefore includes at least the first possibility mentioned above.

---

[32] Such men also ignorantly assume all ancient civilisations to be composed of 'primitives', owing to the scientistic dogma called 'evolutionism'.

When it comes to the second possibility, we have to remember that in Hinduism the word 'soul' is used as a translation for immortal Atma, whereas in Abrahamic traditions and in our culture generally the soul refers to the individuality, especially the mind associated with a body. What is born can (and must) die. What is never born never dies. Hell and death as finality are definitely included in the ancient Egyptian tradition. The doctrine is very solidly held within Christianity even if discussion is avoided in modern times; it is held not only within the moral exoteric side of it but also in the teaching narratives of Jesus and St. Paul. Perhaps the most sublime example is in the words of Jesus recorded by John, 15: 1–7:

> I am the true vine, and my Father is the husbandman.
>
> Every branch in me that beareth not fruit he taketh away: and every branch that beareth fruit, he purgeth it, that it may bring forth more fruit.
>
> Now ye are clean through the word which I have spoken unto you.
>
> Abide in me, and I in you. As the branch cannot bear fruit of itself, except it abide in the vine; no more can ye, except ye abide in me.
>
> I am the vine, ye are the branches: He that abideth in me, and I in him, the same bringeth forth much fruit: for without me ye can do nothing.
>
> If a man abide not in me, he is cast forth as a branch, and is withered; and men gather them, and cast them into the fire, and they are burned.
>
> If ye abide in me, and my words abide in you, ye shall ask what ye will, and it shall be done unto you.

Christ Jesus says here that he is the vine, which is life, and God in heaven is the keeper of the vine. This 'life' is not nature as such but the Real, Atma, whose messenger is the Word of God and the Holy Spirit. To hear that word is to be purged of ignorance concerning the true nature of things by the *jnana-svarupa*, pure knowledge, and the essence of what is real and true. One must abide in that truth, not in an afterlife or a time to come, but now, while living life in the flesh. The analogy of the branches and the vine is like that of the pot and the clay it is made of. The pot only exists relatively, by name and form. When it is seen to be made of clay and nothing but clay, then clay remains and is not even the cause of the pot. Without that Self-Realisation the branch, or the body or pot, is broken and has no further existence. The fruit that is referred to is *jnana-svarupa*, the essential knowledge of what is real. By abiding to the truth, the word of God that is Christ, anything that is desired will be granted—exactly as is the case with the Hindu Mahadevi. The best thing to desire is *jnana-svarupa*, the pure knowledge, for in that alone is freedom.

So we have this possibility of death as finality in the ancient Egyptian, the Greek and probably in some aspects of the Orphic and Persian traditions as well as Christianity, as clearly shown in the text from John and elsewhere. The latter, however, excluded the doctrine of transmigration altogether presumably to avoid all the complexity that comes with that, not to mention that a simplistic notion of that nullifies the need for salvation thus neutralising the teaching of Jesus. The doctrine of transmigration is complex, resting on a cosmological application and development of metaphysics. It cannot be put across in simple terms without risk of distortion, for example, modern 'reincarnationism'. The Neoplatonist Macrobius expressed a view of the Hermetic text, 'Descent of the Soul from the Height of Cosmos to the Depth of Earth', that seems on the face of it closer to that of Hinduism.[33] He asserts the soul's indestructibility, where the worst that can happen appears to be an indefinite duration in a dormant condition akin to the deep or dreamless sleep:

And this is the difference between terrene bodies and supernal—I mean those of the heaven and stars and of the other elements [apart from those of earth]—that the latter are summoned upwards to the abode of the soul, and are worthy of immunity from death [that is immortality] from the very nature of the space in which they are and their imitation of sublimity. The soul, however, is drawn down to these terrene bodies; so it is thought to die when it is imprisoned in the region of things fallen and in the abode of death. Nor should it cause distress that we have so often spoken of death in connection with the soul that we have declared to be superior to death. For the soul is not annihilated by what is called its death, but is only buried for a time; nor is the blessing of its perpetuity taken from it by its submersion for a time, since when it shall have made it worthy to be cleansed clean utterly of all contagion of its vice, it shall once more return from body to the light of Everlasting Life restored and whole.

One must first be aware that the ancient Greek word for the human soul is *psyche* (φυχη), often regarded as a 'spark' of the *pneuma* (πνευμα), of which the direct Latin equivalent is Spirit. Some have the notion that it is a kind of 'force of nature' that gives form to 'matter', and so it is present even in non-sentient objects. All this is deplorably vague and it would be fruitless trying to explain what is already obfuscated by the very use of the terms involved. However, Macrobius is clear enough even if he puts this in simple language.

---

[33] See pp. 73–76, 'Alexandrian Gnosticism', *Metamorphosis*.

The key to it, and one that fits well with the unified doctrine of Hinduism as set forth by Guénon, is that the bodily soul, as defined by her elemental or lower nature, must rise upward to the subtle abode so that immortality is a possibility.[34] This owes to the 'very nature of the space in which they are', that is to say, the souls have undergone a change of state to a higher one—which also signifies a death to the previous state. The 'imitation of sublimity' is most interesting, as it corresponds to the qualification for immortality gained by ritual, devotional and yoga practices, including meditation, for example.[35] Immortality is to be distinguished from the goal of Advaitan and yoga practice called *moksha*, 'deliverance', which is final immersion in Brahma Supreme where there is no return to any manifested state of existence. The realm of immortality, when effective and not 'virtual' or by 'imitation', is a higher state of being in the abode of the Gods or the celestial sphere, typified by the Sanskrit *amrita*, called *ambrosia* by the Greeks. The imitation of sublimity is typified by the Journey of the Soul in various traditions, by which ignorance is removed like so many veils, by degrees. Initiation is also regarded, in its primary form, as a kind of death and a new birth into a life of spirit. This is called the 'second birth' in our book:[36]

> Death came into the world so that man could receive the spiritual knowledge of the True Will—the flame of love that burns within his heart, his real identity.

Man's real identity is Atma. Atma and Brahma are one. That is the Supreme Identity. The Advaitan answer to the question, 'Why did death come into the world' would be something like 'Maya—which is ignorance'. Through the covering of *maya* upon Brahma, we believe that Atma is one and the same as the body and mind. At the beginning of the Advaitan path we have to get rid of that false notion. The sense of the quoted sentence from our book is kinder than the shock tactics sometimes used by Sri Shankaracharya. It gives in as few words as possible the *meaning and purpose of life or existence*, which necessarily includes death as certainty, as obtaining freedom through spiritual knowledge. The seers and sages have devoted their lives to helping others obtain this freedom down the ages, for thousands of years. While that proves nothing to the sceptic, it is self-evident to the one that is qualified—that is to say, the knowledge that is the goal itself is latent within them.

---

[34] See *Man and His Becoming according to the Vedānta*, Chapter 19.

[35] See Guénon, Chapter 21 [*ibid*].

[36] *Law of Thelema* [ibid].

# Mantra and Yantra

The *mantra* is extremely important in all initiatic traditions as it is the primary means of conveying *diksha* or 'initiation' within the Orders or groups. Various meanings of the Sanskrit term also include 'consecration', 'preparation' and most interestingly, 'new vision', as seeing and knowledge often have the same meaning. When the guru gives a mantra to a *sadhaka*, it is called *japa* as that implies continuous repetition. While that is not the only use of the mantra, *japa* is valuable as a means of controlling the mind and stabilising the knowledge, and can be very efficacious as a support to meditation. The word or phrase can itself be the object of meditation.

The whole question of *diksha* is contentious and some prefer not to discuss the subject at all, which is understandable. One should certainly not discuss one's personal mantra. Very often the same mantra will be given to a group; it is still 'personal' when it has been conferred, even if used by all the followers of a particular guru. Why is *diksha* contentious? Very often novices will pester us for *japa* or *diksha* when they have read or heard about it somewhere and sense its importance. However, that feeling does not take account of their readiness to receive it, especially in the real initiatic sense. Impatience is a clear indication of unworthiness, although there is no reason at all why it should not be requested. In so far as it really can transmit initiation then once received it is permanent, and this is why it has been said that no member of an Order can ever leave it, since it is an integral part of being. Those who do leave an Order, as of course happens frequently, especially in the volatile times we live in today, were never truly members so their departure is no different than someone dissociating from any profane club, association or society. Even if initiation were given, they would not have received it.

This brings up a very important question regarding initiation, in whatever way it is given. We will not discuss here the absurdity of 'self-initiation', which is very popular in neo-spiritualism, and will only state here that it is an oxymoron arising from sheer ignorance. Initiation must be transmitted from one who has knowledge of more than a theoretical order, or if not, then at least from one that has received authorisation to initiate from within an Order. Initiation, as we have said, may be given sometimes but not received. Likewise a seed may be cast upon stony ground and so will not flourish.

At the highest level *diksha* is no less than what is called guru *darshana*, where the *samadhi* of the guru is transferred to the practitioner at least temporarily—in which case they have to work on it of course. There are other cases where the person may receive a spiritual influence but owing to their lack of preparedness, its effect is detrimental—although this is usually temporary and it is known that sometimes the power has been subsequently removed by the guru. In such a case, they were not able to withstand the direct transference from the mind of a Brahma-jnanin. It will then become apparent that the giving of a mantra or *diksha* is far more than the practice within the Order of the Golden Dawn where a seasonal 'password' is given, or in some later derivatives of that, where the Neophyte has to figure out a 'secret word' from a code given in the ritual.[37]

A real mantra is never merely invented or made up. The word or phrase will often be one well known from the *Gita* or *Upanishads*, for example, in which case the question arises as to how then can it be in any way 'secret' or indeed personal? It is special because it has been given in the way we have indicated. It is not merely a word; there is power behind it, which is the power of transmission. The guru will also give personal instruction in how to pronounce it and how to use it, which may be different according to the individual.

The secret then is not in a word itself, as is the case with *shruti* ('direct') texts. This is further explained by the *bija mantra*, where not only a word is given but also a deity, called Ishta Devata, the 'chosen deity'. The mantra in this case is linked to the deity and usually a name of the deity is included, as with the much celebrated Om Nama Shiva-ya. There are countless examples in scripture and in hymns of praise. The most important of all of them is Om or AUM as it is a name of Brahma and much else besides.[38]

The three letters A, U, M are merged into one figure. The *chandra-bija* is at the top, which literally means 'moon and dot (or point)'. All mantras include what is also called the *bija-nada*, which is indicative of subtle sound, not uttered physically. The *bija* 'point' is placed over the mantric word to indicate this.

---

[37] For example, using the Western colour correspondences to the paths of the Tree of Life in the King Scale: blue, yellow, orange-yellow, emerald green, blue-black: MABYN (בּמאין), sometimes rendered without the *yod*.

[38] One should refer, in the first instance, to the *Mandukya Upanishad*, which is the authoritative treatise on AUM.

It is for the same reason—of the very subtle nature of this sound—that AUM is referred to in the Vedas indirectly, as Pranava, which is AUM or Brahma Nirguna.[39] This can be taken to mean, 'a boat that carries us away from world illusion and to the Real'. This is further indicated by the moon and point.

It is often said in books or literature that mantras are to be sounded aloud with the voice. While this is sometimes done, it is not the way to enter the mystery of the *bija-nada*. It is therefore best to utter the word silently. In the highest form of the *nada*, it is not uttered at all, not even mentally, but is heard though not with the ears or even the inward sense of hearing. In this case, what is actually experienced is completely indescribable. There are lesser degrees of this, which amount to more indirect forms of knowledge.

The *yantra*, 'image', is also used extensively, and there are countless examples even within Hinduism, let alone neo-spiritualism where symbols are invented as often as they are drawn from a valid tradition. Apart from these—some of which can be effective—the best are no doubt to be found within the ancient Egyptian hieroglyphs. Some of the most effective within the Tantras, and which are also very well known, also happen to be the simplest, for example the point within a triangle:

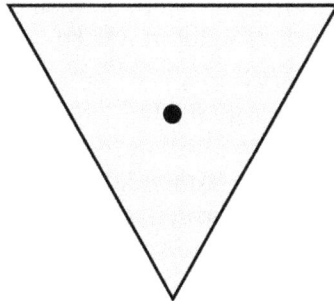

The purpose of this is to meditate, using the *bindu* in the centre as the focal point. Such a *yantra* should preferably be hand drawn and painted by the *sadhaka*. While it can be meditated on externally, as with the mantra it is best when it is transferred to the subtle sense of vision in the first instance. After that, depending on the skill of the operator, the image itself is lost and the real knowledge of the symbol is known directly.

---

39 Thus repetition of the sacred AUM is called Pranava Japa.

Another form of *yantra* is the image of the Ishta Devata. This is used in combination with the *bija mantra*. Traditionally, the idea is to build the image of the deity imaginatively in as much detail as possible. In practice, some are better at this than others, and in fact it is not really essential, especially as the idea is not to stay with the imagination; ideally, the created 'picture' is replaced by the vision of the deity, which is not at all the same thing as imagining it. Although it is not in any way a supreme realisation or something of that order, there are 'degrees' or levels of reality and the vision is of a higher order generally than mere visualisation. This practice is also part of what is called Ishvara Pranidhāna in the *Yoga-Sutras*.

Finally, a word should be said regarding the use of *bija mantra* images and sounds associated with the chakras. There is much of this written about in popular books and elsewhere, and that removes such practices entirely from their traditional use, so we will not give here a list of them. One might gain the impression, even from what might appear to be authoritative sources that the use of mantras extends no further than a means of helping with bodily health or psychological problems. In fact, using them ignorantly in the ways often suggested can be harmful—often the best thing that can happen is that nothing happens at all. Why is this? The methods are ancient and while the main use of these was spiritual, that does not mean that a spiritual influence will have a beneficial effect on one that uses them without knowledge and without a guru to guide them.

Even in tradition, mantras can be used for material purposes and this is not necessarily illegitimate but obviously there is ignorance prevailing in the person using them in this way, exactly as in the case of magical talismans. Our recommendation is to use the mantra and *yantra* for spiritual purposes, which means knowing the Real as the ultimate goal.

# Meditation

In modern times, the science of yoga has become separated from its spiritual purpose. All focus is placed upon the physicality of the yoga postures (*mudras*), breathing techniques and so forth. These were only added to Hatha Yoga when the sages wished to make a complete science of yoga, but were never intended to be separated from meditation or the goal, which is 'union with God'.

In the subtle human body tradition has it there are two forces at work, often symbolised by two serpents, called *ida* and *pingala* in Sanskrit, or personified as Isis and Nephthys in Egypt.[40] These are likened to the solar and lunar force, the Sun and the Moon. Through their interactions we are able to perform all functions. We can live, breathe, eat and think, for example, by virtue of them. At various times one or the other force is dominant. When they are equilibrated, through yoga for example, it becomes possible to raise consciousness to the higher or supra-human states. This is brought about through the means of a 'central canal' called *sushumna* in Sanskrit, which has its equivalent in the central column of the Tree of Life or the trunk of the world tree in various cultures. The Shakti or living power, personified as a goddess of the same name, is able to rise upward along the path of the *sushumna*. This is facilitated by the *pranayama* or inward and outward breath in the yoga practice, combined with upward aspiration and sometimes the use of various images (*yantras*) and sounds (*mantras*).

The primary aim of the yoga practice is withdrawal of the senses from the physical body (and mind) to the subtle body (and psyche). The goal of the working is then to push beyond the psychic realm altogether, so even the subtle senses are withdrawn or assimilated. This alone makes possible the *moksha* ('liberation') of Laya Yoga when carried to its ultimate. Sushumna ends at the top of the skull (*brahmarandra*) but continues through a 'solar ray', which must be followed to its source.

Mention is made of these technicalities as it is helpful to know them, but it is not necessary, and not even advisable, to go into such detail if you are a beginner at meditation. Keep it simple and in that case avoid 'chakra meditations' you might have learned elsewhere, especially if you are doing meditation without guidance.

---

[40] The chakras do not exist in the physical anatomy. When they are 'located' in various parts of the body, it is to serve as analogy, not literal fact.

## 0. Preparations

Wear loose fitting clothes that will not restrict the body in any way—a single robe is the ideal. In our rituals we orient towards the North. Other traditions orient towards the East. Arrange your chair or seat—the place where you will sit—so it faces North. It is preferable to use the same place for your meditation and to arrange regular times for the practice. Furniture and other trappings are not by any means essential but it can help to use candle light and a very small pinch of incense or fragrant oil—in which case avoid the flowery essences and use only the highest quality woods and gums, or their essences.

**1.** Salute the North by raising both hands (level with the brows), placing them together in the characteristic prayer or *namashka* gesture then bringing them down to the heart level while bowing the head for a moment.

**2.** Assume the seated Egyptian Godform *asana*. For Westerners, meditation is best done seated, similar to the way Egyptian gods are depicted when enthroned. Sit comfortably on a chair with your back straight but not tense. Your feet are kept flat on the floor; your knees and hips should be straight but comfortably aligned. Place the palms of your hands flat down upon your thighs. Your head should be facing straight ahead even with closed eyes. The art is to keep perfectly still.[41]

**3.** Pranayama, control of breath: This does not include counting of breath or breathing with one nostril closed. It does not include holding the breath. Breathe deeply and slowly, in through the nostrils and out through the mouth. Breathing is from the diaphragm not the throat, and must be deep but natural, never tense or strained. The idea is to maintain the relaxed breathing throughout the meditation. The rhythm of the breathing should be like the slow rising and falling of the sea. With persistence, you will find your own rhythm.

**4.** Pratyahara: withdrawal of the senses from their sense objects. This and the next, *dharana*, are worked together. In the usual or ordinary case, the mind chases after the senses, with their input providing countless distractions, keeping the mind enthralled and passing from one object to another. Dharana 'concentration' means that the mind has first willed 'silence', and the senses are obedient.

---

[41] If you are able to sit comfortably and without strain in a lotus or half-lotus on the floor or a mat, then by all means do so. We need to keep still, with a straight back and head, and comfortably so the body is not a distraction.

**5.** Dharana: now that the body and mind are calm and still, it is possible to concentrate the mind upon the object of meditation. There are various degrees to this kind of concentration. The novice will find it easiest to practice a form of contemplation. With this, thoughts are allowed but they must relate directly to the meditation object. The Sanskrit term is *vichara*, 'following'. For example an object can be a 'thing', which fills space, it either has movement or it is motionless. After that there are qualities such as colour, heat or coolness and so on. Any other thoughts or feelings are dismissed and not dwelled on. The mind is controlled; it is not allowed to wander.

The more advanced meditation is where the object is held in the mind and all thoughts about it are suppressed. The Sanskrit term for this is *nirvichara*, literally, 'without having thoughts'. Real *dharana* concentration is when the object is held like an unwavering flame.

**6.** Dhyana: when single-pointed concentration has to some extent been achieved, *dhyana* or real meditation is possible. Here, there is a 'flow of knowledge' of the object, but it must be clear that this is not any ordinary kind of knowledge. It means that the engrossment is such with the prolonged concentration—without falling asleep or into a vacuous state—that thought has been eliminated and something like pure consciousness is being approached.

**7.** Closing: Stand up. Repeat the *namashka* 'naming the space' as done at the beginning and add: AUM. Peace be upon all creatures and men.

It should go without saying by now that real meditation takes a great deal of effort and persistence, especially in the early stages when a regular practice is being established. It is not something you can try out every so often and expect to get some sort of result from it. A great deal of what people call 'meditation' nowadays is nothing of the sort. It is not about being quiet or sitting comfortably with a lighted candle or two, with soft music playing in the background. It is not a 'relaxation therapy' although over time you will gain benefits from a serious spiritual practice. In the above simple description we have only mentioned five out of the Ashtanga 'eight limbs'. The first two, the abstentions and observances, cannot be dispensed with. The last, *samadhi* or 'union of subject and object' is the primary goal of yoga. This can take a long time. Even *dhyana*, the true meditation, can take a long time and most persons find it difficult to achieve.

In the above steps we have used the term 'object' for the focus of the concentration. This is sometimes called the meditation 'subject' but really the 'subject' is your own conscious awareness. In *samadhi*, the subject and object are one, without separation. The purpose of all meditation at the outset is to fully realise that all things, all objects, thoughts and imaginings whatsoever are experienced by your mind and senses. There is no 'objective universe' that is not experienced—this is something beyond all argument. Yoga can take us much further even than that. In the yoga of Patañjali, objects can be many and various but they most often begin with *tattvas*, 'elementary principles' such as earth, water, fire, air and ether or *akasha*. It is beyond the scope of this work to go into all the details of that but the best kind of meditation object in general, providing the person is devotionally inclined, is the Ishta Devata, 'chosen deity'.[42] It is very efficacious as a prelude to the real concentration to imaginatively place oneself in a special location, temple or shrine and to make offerings to the deity of flowers, incense, libations and so forth.

Ritual is frequently overlooked by those whose learning is solely from books, without affiliation to an Order. We have given here a minimum of rituals, kept simple, but more can be done. A *mudra* is more than a mere gesture, such as placing the first and second fingers together in a sign of blessing and raising the hand up to heaven. It can be that but the word *mudra* means more than one thing, including 'attitude', 'seal'. It is not the gesture or form of the body alone but the whole attitude or disposition of the practitioner that is involved. Ritual, when properly done, is a form of external or objectified meditation. The *mudras* place a 'seal', a deep impression on the mind and body, and more than that, when well done they are much liked by the deities and this attracts their real presence.

In the next chapter we will discuss the Eight Limbs of Yoga, but from an Advaitan point of view. Then we will give some hints as to various ways that the practice can be made really effective, especially by placing the image of the deity in the heart lotus and merging the 'I' identity with it, or the effulgence that comes about when concentration is sustained.

---

[42] The *Yoga-Sutras* of Patañjali are gone into in some considerable detail and depth in our two books, *Thunder Perfect Gnosis—Intellectual Flower of Mind* and *Metamorphosis—Hermetic Science and Yoga Power*.

# Ashtanga Yoga

The Eight Limbs of Yoga, variously adapted from the *Yoga-Sutras* of Patañjali, are well known to most persons that have even a passing knowledge of this subject. Here we will take another look at Ashtanga Yoga, but this time from the Advaitan Non-dualist point of view.[43]

The first limb is called *Yamas*: harmlessness; truthfulness; non-stealing; continence; non-covetousness. We will not repeat here the more usual interpretation of these, which has been adequately (if not by any means exhaustively) dealt with.[44] All this concerns our relations with other people and all else in the world. It sets a general standard of behaviour or conduct—and also a very high one when it is really followed through; one is meant to meditate on these. The difference is that if we know that our Self is truly Brahma, all this becomes perfectly natural and nothing at all should be in any way forced. If it is forced and imposed, either from someone else or from our selves, it only serves to reinforce the dualistic delusion. If suppression leads to psychopathology, the abstentions are worse than useless. The one purpose of *practicing* abstentions—until they are realised as completely natural to the being—is to know the Self as Brahma and that everything is (in reality) Brahma.

The second limb is called *Niyamas*: cleanliness; contentment; fiery aspiration; self-study; self-surrender to the path, which is God. By 'self-study' is not meant any kind of psychological examination. It is the enquiry into the true nature of the Self, which must lead to the knowledge of the Self as Brahma. The rest are all to serve that end and meditation will prove it as self-evident.

Then with the third limb begins the actual practice of yoga and meditation: *Asana*, seated posture. This is already well known, and we favour a particular method called the Egyptian Godform, seated as though enthroned, and so forth—we will not describe it in detail here. However, we have always agreed with Advaita on this as well as many other points, and it is all about the 'Seat (*asana*) of Brahma'. The sole purpose of taking up seated posture is to know the Self as Brahma. It is also interesting to note that the Sanskrit *asana* and Egyptian Iset are similar sounding and mean exactly the same thing.

---

[43] See 'Patañjali Eight Limbs of Yoga', *Thunder Perfect Gnosis*.
[44] Ibid, pp. 153–155.

However, anything that is uncomfortable or distracting is clearly no use in getting to the goal of yoga. The general instructions are to be followed, to keep a straight back, though not rigidly, and to keep the eyes closed and head straight and so forth. The purpose of any *asana* is to quickly be able to forget the body.

The fourth limb as given by Patañjali is *Pranayama*, control of breath. There are various means of doing this but neither Advaita nor we have ever advocated the 'four-fold breath' with counting, or the method of closing one nostril and then the other. In any case if it is done then it should only be done with a knowledgeable Hatha Yoga instructor (as it is derived from Hatha Yoga). The real understanding of the control of breath is this: breathing in is AUM. That is to say, we are assimilating the knowledge of the Self as Brahma. Breathing out is to declare all that is Maya or non-self, and yet at the same time we must understand that ultimately Maya too is one with Brahma, only she has the power to delude us with the appearance of all, which seems not to be Brahma but in reality is!

The fifth limb of yoga is *Pratyahara*, withdrawal of senses. In some respects, this cannot be done without the next step (*dharana*), but it is placed here first as it would be no use concentrating on any sense object that happened to occur to us. The senses are withdrawn from the sense objects so we can concentrate on the one thing, which of course, as by now will become obvious, is Brahma. Now when we do the Samyama Yoga meditation in order to gain the discriminating knowledge of an object, whatever it might be, it needs never to be forgotten that the whole purpose of this is to know the Self as Brahma, or *sat-chit-ananda* pure being, consciousness and bliss.

The sixth limb of yoga is *Dharana*, concentration, fixation. We are already concentrating so as to withdraw the senses from their objects, so *dharana* specifically means here a level of engrossment in the object of meditation is attained. There is still a subject and an object, a knower and thing known, but engrossment is such that we are beginning to lose the difference, at least for moments at a time.

That leads to the seventh limb of yoga, which is *Dhyana*, true meditation with sustained concentration. Meditation only begins here! This can come as a surprise to some people who imagine that they are already doing meditation without covering any of the other steps mentioned here. There is a 'flow of knowledge' about the object, described as 'nectar' or like an unbroken stream of honey.

It can be seen then that *dhyana*, when sustained, can move effortlessly into *Samadhi* (union with God—the goal, which is yoga). This is the primary goal of yoga, and implies total engrossment or union. The word 'union' is misleading, because it can still imply there are two things, whereas in the highest *samadhi*, called Nirvikalpa, there is no longer any difference; there are not two things but all is one: Atma and Brahma are *One and not two*, which is the meaning of Advaita Vedanta.

# Non-dual Raja Yoga

P ractice, as we have constantly asserted, is indispensible if we are to gain more than theoretical knowledge. Strange to relate, a great number of persons study Advaita Non-dualism and form the notion that it does not have practices other than reading books and thinking on the teaching therein. That could not be further from the truth. If it were true then there would be no Advaitan monasteries in India, only libraries. Having said that, it will be admitted that the techniques of Advaita Vedanta remain something of a secret to this day. This is for more than one reason, and is not for the sake of secrecy alone, the retaining of special knowledge, but has to do with the nature of the subject itself. The *Upanishads*, which is the basis of Advaitan teaching, is concerned with non-perceptible reality, something so alien to modern thinking as to be completely out of the reach of those conditioned by its severe limitations.

At the very beginning of this book we explained the qualifications for Advaita Vedanta. This is obviously exclusive to those who are in possession of at least a modicum of the qualifications, so becoming a practitioner is not something that 'anyone' can do. For this reason, of the special or non-ordinary nature of the intelligence required for knowledge of Non-dual reality, a 'secret' can be disclosed openly in writing or speech and it will remain to all intents and purposes as though it were rolled up in a scroll, bound tightly and sealed.[45]

By now the reader will certainly want to know if we are going to reveal such secrets of practice here? The answer is yes and no at the same time—which will no doubt infuriate those who entirely lack the qualifications we have referred to. Let us make it clear before we go further: while the techniques as such are enough to fill many volumes of books, and they do, it is how they are put together that renders them effective or not. Only knowledge destroys ignorance. All that can be written down is no more than ordinary knowledge, yet if even that is approached ignorantly, the state of unknowing remains. If we were to stand in a completely dark room it would make no difference what words we sound forth; the room will remain as dark as the soul of night herself until we strike a match and flood it with light.

---

[45] The ancient Egyptian hieroglyphic determinative for estotericism is exactly what is described here—a rolled up scroll, tied and sealed.

The Advaitans, going back to the 'first', Adi Shankaracharya, took a great deal from the other orthodox *darshana* schools of thought, most especially the *Yoga-Sutras* of Patañjali, otherwise known as Ashtanga Yoga—'yoga of eight limbs'. Advaita tends to simplify the methods of such yoga while at the same time the understanding of it is coming from a higher level or degree. If the *Yoga-Sutras* and the commentaries are followed through to their ultimate—something that only a few yogins of exceptional ability will ever be able to do— we become self-enclosed or isolated, as a star in the night (*kaivalya*). At least, that is how it looks in theory, and that also leads to the idea that yoga is 'dualistic', since the perfected Self or *purusha* is apart from all else.[46] The mind has been 'arrested', shut down almost totally, so that separation is maintained between this true Self and all the universe of appearances, called *maya*. Whether the isolationism is true or not of the rare case of one that has attained *kaivalya*, what is certainly true is that Advaita goes one or two steps further than Ashtanga Yoga. It might seem to be enough that at the height of yoga one realises that one is truly Atma, which is called *purusha* in the *Yoga-Sutras*, but Advaita provides us with a fail-safe against any possibility of isolationism. How does Advaita do this? Advaitan Self-Realisation is in two stages. The first follows almost exactly the way of Patañjali Yoga, where one must practice until one truly sees and knows that 'I am not this body; I am not this mind'. This is absolutely necessary otherwise the aspirant will be trapped into the ordinary human condition, where due to ignorance of the true state of affairs the Self is mistakenly identified with the body and mind, alone and separate in an indefinitely vast and incomprehensible universe filled with other creatures and things.[47]

---

[46] This theory was adopted to a certain extent by the German philosopher Leibniz, and this was in turn taken up, and no doubt made subject to further distortion, through certain Western occultists—but indeed, the 'monadic' notion seems to be one that is peculiarly desirable to the Western or modern mentality, since it permits a kind of sovereignty to the human ego. That is not at all what was intended by the ancient sages, but once in the hands of those whose minds have been deformed by the insidious influence of a modern education it easily becomes so.

[47] Conventional science can give no relief at all to this miserable condition, in fact it makes things much worse. Science measures all things that can be measured; it produces theories that constantly change but knows nothing of reality beyond that which can be experienced by the mind and senses and even that, as it has no basis in a higher principle, fails to relieve suffering.

The next stage of Advaitan Self-Realisation is to turn this around, to reverse the position completely. The first stage has to be fully realised, however, otherwise we are still under the delusion that the real Self is no more than a collection of objects formed by the mind and senses. So having realised Atma is not the body and not the mind, not any perceived object, one is then able to realise that the Self is in fact Brahma Nirguna or Brahma Supreme, and that the entire universe of appearances is the product of Maya, who is no different from Brahma as the Shakti magical power behind all phenomena.

To pass to the second stage, we have to know the Self as Atma, without conditions or any determinations. We have to know this for a fact, beyond any doubt. Continuous practice is needed, supported by study of the relevant texts along with contemplation or reflective thought and an unfailing vigilance of discrimination (*viveka*). Yoga meditation is definitely required, and while Advaita understands *samadhi* (union) somewhat differently than as it is put in the yoga commentaries, it happens to be the case that one should first gain technical and experiential familiarity with the methods of Patañjali. Once the discipline, including intellective discrimination, has been followed to the point of knowing the I-sense, then further teaching can be given regarding the Advaitan next step. Until that stage has been reached it will not make any difference what 'exercises' we do. However, what we will give here is something that anyone with a reasonable intellectual capacity should be able to accomplish without risk of injury to their being. It is also proven to be effective with intermediate practitioners, to assist them in getting further along the way towards that next step.

This is actually consisting of two distinct practices, where one is supportive of the other: while there are many different practices within Ashtanga Yoga, the one that is most generally efficacious is where the sense of 'I', the ego sense of self that most persons imagine to be located in their head, behind their eyes, is relocated to the heart lotus, which is more or less in the centre of the chest, not the heart as a physical organ. One must then endeavour to place all the awareness in the heart lotus, called Brahma Loki, 'Seat of Brahma' (literally 'World of Brahma'). This is not the *anahatha* chakra as familiar to those who have read about Laya Yoga or even practiced it. It is envisioned as being either within the *anahatha* as a small shrine or 'cave', or otherwise slightly below, above or within that chakra.

We must also remember in this that consciousness is not in any case located anywhere, so all places are analogous. The analogous locations are a matter of convenience but over thousands of years they have been proven to be effective.

> For you are born of the noble spring—how can I speak
> Of the holm oak that's rooted above
> The hollow in the rock where your
> Clear babbling waters run down?[48]

In more than one esoteric tradition we do not ascend Mount Meru or Abiegnus, or by whatever name it is called, to the summit.[49] That is to say, the secret is to climb half way up the mountain and from there we go into the interior, by entering a cave or hollow. Only then are we are able to complete the Divine Journey of the Soul. What do we do when we have wended our way to the exact centre of the mountain? We meditate—and by that is not meant merely sitting quietly and trying to calm the mind. Meditation involves great effort at the outset as it involves withdrawal of the senses (*pratyahara*), concentration (*dharana*) and sustained engrossment or one-pointedness (*dhyana*).

However, this present work is in no way intended to be a manual of practical instructions.[50] What is important to know is that yoga includes a method called Ishvara Prānidhana, 'devotion to God (or Shakti)'. In this, the deity is placed as in this shrine of the heart and then the ego sense is identified with the deity. Obviously this only works with those inclined towards *bhakti* or devotion, which is often though not accurately described as a religious attitude. However, this greatly falicitates what comes next for those who are able to do it.

The purpose of the second method, which follows here, is to defeat an obstruction that often afflicts those who try to meditate to the point of real yoga union, where the separation between subject and object is completely fused into one. They will find it impossible not to see the object of their meditation, whatever that object may be, as something quite distinctly apart from their self. While it is true that objects of the mind are not the real Self, that which illuminates them is none other than that Self, called the Witness consciousness.

---

[48] *Odes of Horace*, 3: 13.

[49] It is interesting to note that Mount Abiegnus, from the Neo-Rosicrucian tradition, is etymologically associated with the holm oak. Trees are as much symbolic of initiation as are mountains and caves.

[50] Our treatise on Ashtanga Yoga is spread over two volumes forming the second section of each book: *Thunder Perfect Gnosis—Intellectual Flower of Mind*, and *Metamorphosis—Hermetic Science and Yoga Power*.

Why does this difficulty arise as an obstacle for practitioners? It is because we are very visually oriented and the sense of sight, in the conventional sense of the word, always means there is a *seer* and a thing that is *seen*.[51] So when we close our eyes to meditate—the fact we close our eyes is taken as understood here—and try to be 'not seeing with the eyes', we are inclined to continue to form objects with our inner sense of sight. For example, if we are given an analogy involving the drawing of light or effulgence to a small point what very often happens is the worthy *sadhaka* will find themselves involved in a game of subtle plane pinball! They are still looking at a light, or effulgence, or a point of light, and as soon as they do that then it starts to play tricks; it jumps around, turns into other objects and so forth. But the point of light is an analogy for the awareness of 'I'. We are not meant to be looking at 'I' we are meant to be *experiencing* it— which is what we always do but without thinking about it or realising it at all. The difference is that whereas we usually experience it in an indirect way, where it is simply taken for granted that there is this 'I-sense', this 'me', which is supposedly located in a body, and that body itself located in a vast universe, in meditation we are looking to experience that I-sense and no other thing.

To get round this difficulty caused by the centrality of our sense of vision, which gives us images, location, direction, perspective and all the rest, here is a simple but very powerful technique: close your eyes as usual with meditation and, to begin with, see a small point of light, or even an intense radiance like a small sun. With this part you are still only visualising something, using your inner sight and imagination plus memory. Put that little spot of sunlight right in the back of your head, near the nape of the neck.[52] Now hold that until you can clearly see it steadily with your inner eye. The next stage is to transfer your sense of 'I', your conscious awareness, to that spot of light so you are no longer seeing it because *it is you*. All of you, what you are in so far as you are an individual or separate being, is now that spot of light in the back of your head. You are in that point and all else is outside of it, including your thoughts, memories, external objects and the entire universe. When you are able to do this, if only for a few seconds if you are not an experienced yoga practitioner, you will have realised the pure I-sense as it is termed in Ashtanga Yoga.

---

[51] In ancient languages the words for 'see' and 'seen' also refer to knowledge itself. This gives rise to much confusion.

[52] This has nothing to do with the medulla oblongata or other anatomical details such as given in biology or neurology.

It is generally the aim of the yogin to sustain this, without any thoughts or feelings getting in the way, for quite a long time. Once you are able to do this you will understand better all the teaching of yoga regarding the gross level, *bhutas*, the *pranic* level, the mentality and the higher intellectual principle beyond even the I-sense. You will understand better the teaching of Advaita Vedanta that insists 'I am not this body; I am not this mind'. It is true that if you do this you are still experiencing it in your mind but if you are able to shut down all other thoughts and feelings you will begin to appreciate that 'you' are really something quite other than what is usually supposed.

It is needful to know that this is not Atma; it is the I-sense, which is quite distinct from Atma. We can understand it like this, using one of the well-known analogies used by Sri Shankaracharya. Individuals are likened to many pots or vessels filled with water. Each one of them has a small image of the sun reflected on its surface. Each one is different—some water is cloudy some clear, some water has more movement some is still; some pots are big and some small, and so on. The reflection of the sun is the I-sense, the ego. It is this light that we use to perceive all things in the mind, inclusive of memory, thought and objects based on what we can hear, touch, see, taste and smell. And yet there is only one sun that does not change in any way, and which is the light of Atma in this example. That is the true Self; it is what we really are, if only we can know it. The purpose of Advaita Vedanta is to realise it as fact. Once that truth is known, it is never forgotten but the practice is continued. If there are times we cannot know it directly we use the power of recollection to bring it to mind. In yoga too it is the purpose to maintain this realisation at all times or for as much of the time as possible.

# KUNDALINI YOGA

## RISING TO THE
## THOUSAND-PETALLED LOTUS

# Rising to the Thousand-petalled Lotus

The six chakras or lotuses, plus the one that passes beyond all, are by now very well known to the West thanks to the pioneering work of Sir John Woodroffe ('Arthur Avalon') and his book *The Serpent Power*, which was based on a translation of Tantrik texts that had Laya Yoga for a basis. The *bija mantras* or seed vibrations for the chakras, of which five have a correspondence with the elemental *tattvas* from the Shankya *darshana*, upon which the *Yoga-Sutras* had their basis, were first mentioned in the *Jabala Darshana Upanishad*.[53] Its subject is the *sannyasin*, the one that has renounced all worldly desire, and the 'holy city', which can be an actual city—'the one that Shiva never leaves'—but is really the *purusha* or abode within.

The practice of Ashtanga or Eight-limbed Yoga is integral to the *Jabala Darshana* text. However, even at that time it was made clear that liberation is available to any person regardless of their stage of life, or Ashrama. Of course, 'any person' at that time did not mean that such a science and high spiritual path was open to 'all', without distinction. The four stages of life or Ashramas were and still are to a certain extent embedded in the Sanatana Dharma ('eternal law' or 'ordinance') of India. The first stage is the student of the Vedas, who at an early age takes a vow of celibacy as part of the necessary qualifications, and becomes attached to the house of a guru. The second was the householder, who has the most powerful worldly attachments, as he desires money, material goods, wife, children, property, cattle and so forth. He is heavily weighed down with duties and responsibilities. The third stage is that of the hermit or forest-dweller. The householder, once his duties are fulfilled, can entrust his household to a son and go to live the rest of his life in the forest or on the mountain to devote his self to God or Brahma, often accompanied by his wife. The fourth stage is that of the *sannyasin*, who totally renounces all worldly desires and only wants *moksha* deliverance. There is a song recorded by 'M', the faithful disciple of Sri Ramakrishna:

---

[53] The date of this text is uncertain, as is always the case with ancient scriptures, but it may be as early as the last few centuries BC. One should never assume that such knowledge originated from when it was written down, or that it was the invention of one man. The oral tradition conveyed knowledge for thousands of years peviously.

Awake, Mother! Awake! How long Thou hast been asleep
In the lotus of the Muladhara!
Fulfil thy secret function, Mother:
Rise to the thousand-petalled lotus within the head,
Where mighty Shiva has his dwelling; Swiftly pierce the six lotuses
And take away my grief, O Essence of Consciousness![54]

Chanting the *mantras* alone will not destroy all *karma* but from the Advaitan point of view, he who knows Brahma directly will realise that for him *karma* no longer exists, even while he continues to live a life as a mortal human being. That mortality is only the appearance of things. The one that attains *moksha* (deliverance) knows that he is veritably Brahma and that all else is an appearance.

A word must be said regarding the popularisation of the chakras or lotuses since Woodroffe published his book, *The Serpent Power*. By now, almost everything we might read or hear about isolates certain techniques, completely removing them from all spiritual contexts whatsoever. The modern mentality has no concept at all of the spiritual; it cannot comprehend anything apart from body and mind. Thus we will be given to understand that mantric techniques can be used for the sole purpose of improving one's worldly lot, or for the curing of physical or psychological defects. We will hear that we can 'balance' our chakras and bring about whatever in the world is desired by us. The chakras or lotuses are linked so firmly to physical organs, nerves or the adrenal glands that it is completely forgotten that the lotuses do not exist as physical objects at all. In India, at the time that Woodroffe was researching his study, some gurus regarded the knowledge of the lotuses with absolute contempt, likening them to sweets or flowers sold in the market place to all and sundry by charlatans. Indeed, that view is not far off the mark if we compare it with what has happened with the rise of the New Age and neo-spiritual industry. The aim of the yoga is completely the opposite of that of the peddlers of 'wellbeing'. The first stage in yoga is to realise 'I am not this body; I am not this mind', as we hope to have made very clear in the main content of the present work

[54] *The Gospel of Sri Ramakrishna* as translated by Swami Nikhilananda, p. 242 [Ramakrishna-Vivekananda Centre, New York].

It does not even occur to the millions who practice 'yoga for health' or practice chakra meditations out of a book that what they do and what they teach might be dangerous to the extent that it can be harmful to the being. The techniques are attached to very powerful forces, and these can become active even in the hands of those who are spiritually ignorant and unskilful with yoga. Even those who are skilled in the physical aspect of Hatha Yoga have no idea of what they are dealing with on the subtle level, and if trouble comes they will never suspect it owes to their removing an ancient science entirely from its spiritual meaning, discipline and context.

Yoga is a vast subject. What we give here is no more than a summary of the lotuses, their *mantras* and *yantras*. It is more than enough though for the man of knowledge—that is already proficient in other aspects of Raja Yoga for example, and that is well read in the source texts—to use it for practice. The question then arises, given the potential danger of the profane use of the chakras and *bija mantras* of Laya Yoga, as to why publish this at all? The answer is simple. It is far too late to make amends for the damage done, or to protect fools from their own foolishness. By now thousands of books must be in existence, nearly all of which have sought to make the use of the chakras accessible to all, regardless of qualifications. In fact most of them use the allurement of the *siddhis* or magical powers as a selling point, to the extent that the technical knowledge, once reduced and rendered in the most elementary terms, bears no relation to its original context. It is worthwhile then setting down the basic principles here so that those few that are qualified may benefit from having the record set straight

There is little if anything that can be done to help those ignorant ones who would seek to gain advantage from making material use of the powers locked within the lotuses. We can put it this way: while a saint may enjoy the vision of an angel, when that same angel appears to a sinner he only beholds a terrible and fearsome demon. And if the sinner, as is most often the case, does not have the ability to see such things, and even lacks the conscience to learn of his own errors and make the necessary corrections, then he is in the position of one that has walked into quicksand blindfolded. He sinks, and does not even see what it is that consumes him.

We do not then give here a method for the practice of the Book of the Fifty Gates, as it is termed. We insist that practice requires a sound theoretical basis and an innate love of the Kundalini Shakti, which is not to be thought of as some power held within the body and belonging to the self, as some would like to have it, but is the power of God and verily God. It also requires a qualified teacher or guru. The latter, in the way we mean it, excludes all professionalism. We are in a realm where the qualifications that may be gained in a university are not only irrelevant but might also be a considerable hindrance, even an insurmountable obstacle, owing to the fact that modern education has an effect on the mentality that is, shall we say, far from positive in respect of spirituality.

# The Lotuses of Kundalini Shakti

There are three principal *nadis* or canals for force within the subtle anatomy: *ida*, likened to the sun, *pingala*, likened to the moon, and a central conductor of fire called *sushumna*. The three are sometimes likened to the Pravana, or AUM. Within the *sushumna* by which Kundalini Shakti arises, there are three *granthis* or knots that prevent her upward movement. They are also doors to be opened. Called 'three *lingas*' (Itara Linga) they shine like lightning. Here the power of Shaktimaya is very great. At these points, the Fire, Sun and Moon (*nadis*) converge.

**1.** The Brahma Granthi, located in the *muladhara* chakra, is related to the physical body, to the world of names and forms. The being is here chained to the physical world of appearances, through the ignorance of mistaking it for reality, admitting no higher principle.

**2.** Vishnu Granthi, located between the *manipura* and the *anahatha* chakra, is related to the subtle body and to the world of thoughts, feelings, etc. The being is here chained to the sensual world of desire, dreams and illusions.

**3.** Rudra Granthi, located at the *ajna* chakra, is related to the causal body and to the world of spirit. The knot chains the being by attachment to *siddhis*, the magical powers or the *siddhas*, the magical beings. Essentially, though these are higher worlds, there is still a taint of desire for an individual and separate existence.

## Five Elements (Tattva Bhutas)

The five elements are determinations of the five *tanmatras*; earth from *gandha* (smell), water from *rasa* (taste), fire from *rupa* (sight), air from *sparsha* (touch) and *akasha* from *shabda* (hearing).

## Vision and Voice

When sounding the *bija mantras* for the chakras one visualises the symbol. It is said that the addition of the *ng* sound to the semi-vowels of the Sanskrit alphabet turns them into *bija mantras*. The *ng* sound is nasal, like the elephant's sound, *nishad* or *ni* (one of the notes of the Indian music scale). The letter of the *bija* mantra for each lotus or chakra is placed in the centre of the illustrations. Each rests upon a symbolic animal, which is the power of the *tattva*, in the case of the first five from *muladhara* upwards.

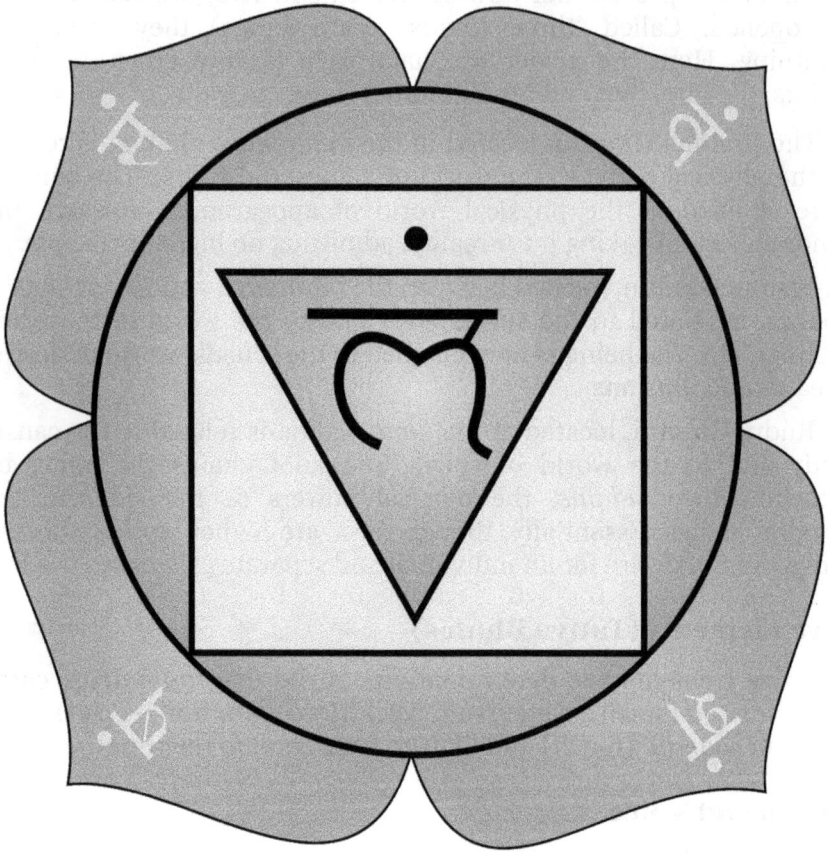

Muladhara Chakra

The petals of each lotus have a Sanskrit letter, fifty in all: four in *muladhara*, six in *svadisthana*, ten in *manipura*, twelve in *anahatha*, sixteen in *vishuddha* and two in *ajna*. Each letter is a Shakti or devi, and a subtle sound *nada*. The word *nada* implies subtle vibration, akin to light, and it is symbolised by the *bija* point or mark above each letter. The sum totality of all the petals is the Mantric Body of Kundalini Shakti. She is both light (*jyotirmayi*) and *mantra* (*mantramayi*). In this, light is regarded as the subtle aspect of her manifestation, while sound or *mantra* is the gross aspect, for example when Japa is done—which is the repetition of a *mantra* as conferred by a guru.

## Muladhara Chakra: Earth; *prithivi*

Muladhara is formed from *mula* meaning 'root' and *adhara* meaning 'foundation or base'; it is the foundation of the seven chakras and is located at the base of the spine in the subtle anatomy. The sense of smell is related to the element of earth and the nose is the sense organ. The earth element is the foundation of body, bones, flesh, skin and hair. The *tattva* of earth or *prithivi* is a yellow square.

The petals on the lotus consist of the letters Vam, Śam, Ṣam, and Sam. The letters in all cases, apart from *ajna*, read clockwise around the lotus. The *bija mantra* for this chakra is LAM sounded as LANG, shown in the centre of the drawing with the *bija* or seed principle above. The *mantra* LANG is focused in the base chakra. When properly produced, the sound LANG excites the *nadis* in *muladhara* and creates a lock that prevents the downward movement of energy. LA is the sound for the earth element and NG is *nada-bindu*, the subtle form of the sound. The *bija mantra* rests on the elephant Airāvata, summarising the qualities of the *tattva*—as is the case with all the symbolic animals of the chakras.

The upward movement of power begins when the sound ANG vibrates in the head. This creates a passage inside the *brahma nadi*— the subtle channel through which Kundalini Shakti, when awakened, moves from *muladhara* to the *sahasrara* chakra. Sounding LANG invokes the power of Indra, King of the Devas and Lord of Heaven. The Shakti is Dakini. There are variations in the names of the deities; Woodroffe gives the Lord here as Brahma and the Shakti as Savitri. Shiva and Shakti are the lingam and triangle. Kundalini is here coiled three and one half times around the Shiva Linga, covering with her head (or mouth) the entrance to the *sushumna* (Brahma-dvāra).

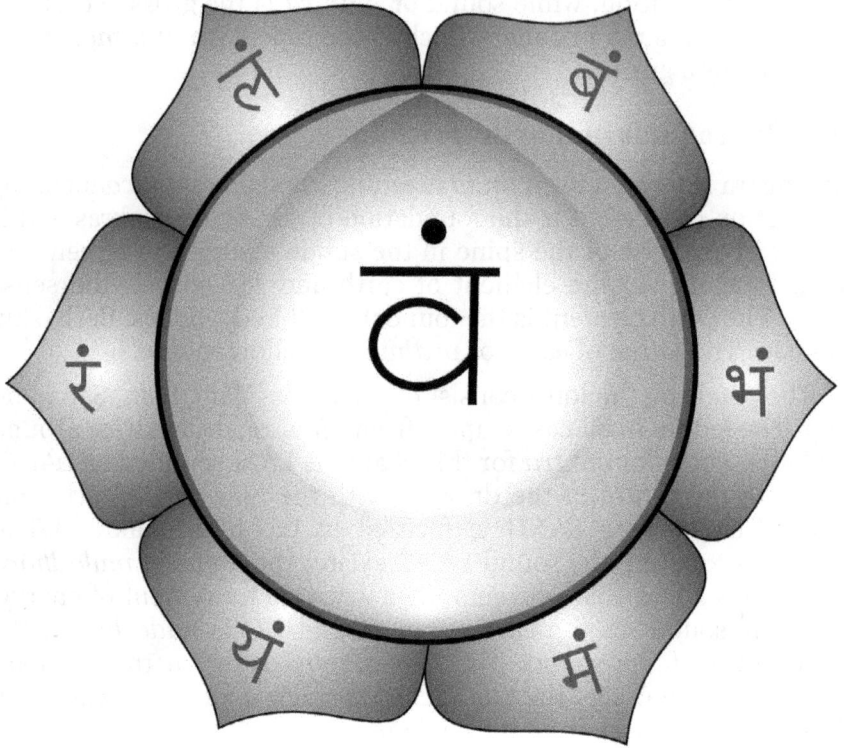

Svadisthana Chakra

## Svadhisthana Chakra: Water; *apas*

Svadhisthana means 'Abode of the Shakti'; it is located in the subtle anatomy at the sacrum. The water element is a determination of the *rasa tanmatra* (taste principal), and the tongue is its sense organ. The *tattva* of water or *apas* is a silver crescent. Whereas the *samskaras* or deep mental impressions from past experience are dormant in *muladhara*, they find expression in the *svadhisthana*, where worldly desire and the sexual impulse are very strong. It is at this level that one might also encounter subtle or astral entities.

The letters drawn on the petals flash like lightning: Bam, Bham, Mam, Yam, Ram, and Lam.

The *bija mantra* for this chakra is VAM sounded as VANG, shown in the centre of the drawing. If produced properly, the sound of this *bija mantra* will influence the flow of *prana* in the *svadhisthana* chakra. The *bija* rests upon a white Makara carrying a noose. The Makara is a type of chimera, somewhat like a dolphin or fish with the head of an alligator.

The power of Varuna, an aspect of Vishnu (sustainer of creation) is present in the *bija mantra* VANG. Varuna is the god of all forms of the water element, particularly the oceans. He wields the conch, mace, wheel and lotus and rides upon an eagle.

The Lord is Hari (Vishnu) and the Shakti is Parvati or otherwise Rakini, of furious aspect, wielding a trident, *vajra*, drum and lotus. When the *bija mantra* VANG is repeated then the *svadhisthana* chakra is purified.

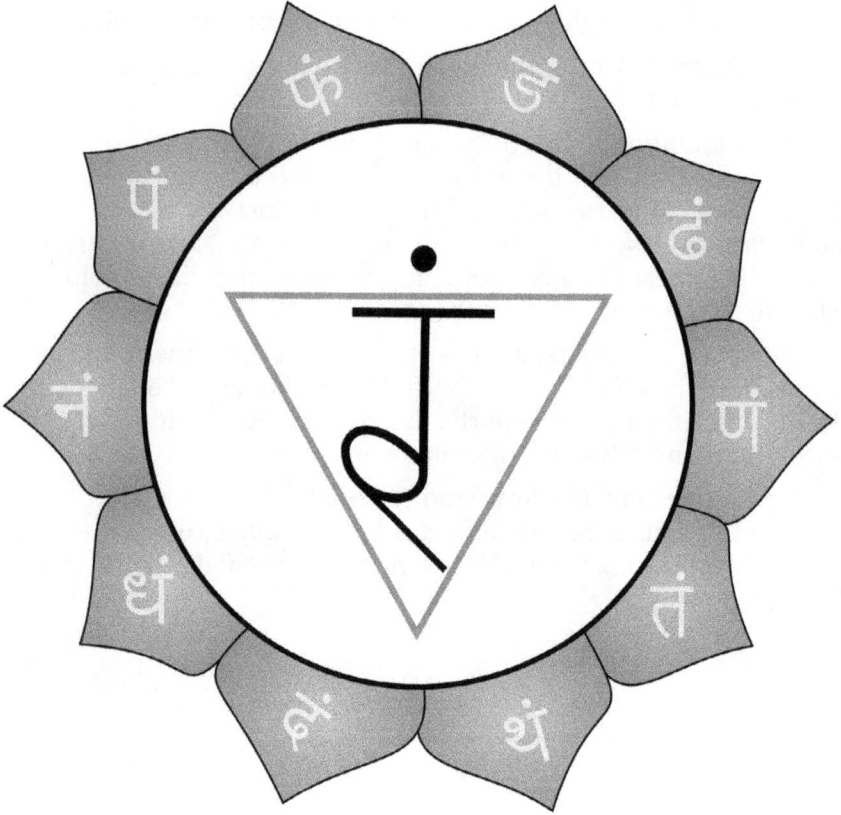

Manipura Chakra

## Manipura Chakra: Fire; *tejas*

Manipura means 'city of jewels'; it is derived from two words *mani* meaning 'jewel' and *pura* meaning 'city'. Manipura is located in the area of the naval in the subtle anatomy. The *manipura chakra* is considered to be the centre of dynamism, energy and willpower, which radiates *prana* throughout the entire subtle body. It is associated with the power of fire, and digestion. It is also associated with the sense of sight or vision.

The letters on the ten petals are: Ďam, Ďham, Ņam, Tam, Tham, Dam, Nam, Pam, and Pham.

The *tattva* of fire or *tejas* is a red triangle. The fire element consists of both heat and light, but the heat is dominant. The fire element is related to the sun, the ruling planet of this chakra. The sun is the source of life in the solar system, and the navel represents the source of life in the body. The fire element in the navel region aids in the digestion and absorption of food, which supplies the whole body with sustenance. The fire element is related to hunger, thirst, sleep, lethargy and radiance (*ojas*). The fire element is purifying and nourishing, yet can also be destructive. If this were not so it could not aid in digestion or, on a subtler level, assimilation of knowledge.

The *bija mantra* for this chakra is RAM and is sounded as RANG, shown in the centre of the drawing. The sound is heard in the navel when repeated in the proper way. The sound RANG increases fire, which enhances assimilation and absorption. The nature of fire is to move upwards and the repetition of this mantra helps the upward movement of Kundalini Shakti.

Agni is the God of Fire and the acceptor of sacrifices. He is shining red, has four arms, holds a *mala* and a spear, and makes the gestures of granting boons and dispelling fear. The ram is the vehicle of Agni and carrier of the *bija mantra* RAM. The Lord is Rudra, smeared with ashes, and the Shakti is Lakini, the Benefactress of All that eats animal food and is bloody. The Shaktis of the higher lotuses beyond *manipura* do not consume the flesh of animals.

Anahatha Chakra

94

## Anahatha Chakra: Air; *vayu*

In Sanskrit the word *anahatha* means 'unbroken, unstruck and unbeaten'. Anahatha Nad is the subtle sound of the celestial realm. The *anahatha* chakra is analogously located near the region of the heart and is as red as a bandhuka flower. Because of its association with touch, it is associated with the skin and with the hands. The *tattva* of air or *vayu* is a blue circle. Vayu is the vital life-giving force (*prana*). It aids the functions of the lungs and heart, circulating fresh oxygen and subtle *prana*. Air is formless and colourless, without smell or taste. Purusha dwells here—hence the 'unstruck sound', or otherwise Jivatma. Here is the Tree of Life that grants all wishes (Kalpatara) and the jewelled Altar (Mañi-pithi) beneath it. It is the place of the Ishta-devata, the 'chosen deity'. Power can pass upwards or downwards. It is 'the great chakra in the heart of all things'. The *anahatha* chakra includes the six-pointed star formed of two triangles, which symbolises Shiva and Shakti. The *anahatha* chakra is associated with love and desire. It is also the Seat of Brahma and here, Atma may be realised as the steady flame of a lamp in a windless place.

The twelve letters are: Kam, Kham, Gam, Gham, Ņam, Cam, Cham, Jam, Jha, Jñam, Ţam, and Ţham.

The *bija mantra* for this chakra is YAM sounded as YANG, shown in the centre of the drawing. The *bija* rests upon a black antelope (swiftness, motion). The *mantra* is focused in the heart chakra. When this sound is perfectly produced true knowledge dawns in the consciousness and the second knot, the Vishnu Granthi, is undone, allowing *prana* to start to flow upward. Sounding the *bija mantra* YANG gives one control over air, *prana* and the breath. The *bija mantra* YANG is the sonic form of the deity Vayu, the Lord of the Air and the Winds. The Lord, as with the first three chakras, is Isha. The Shakti is Rakini, who is depicted as having black skin and two faces with shining tusks. She is otherwise named Kakini, who wears a necklace of human bones, and whose heart is softened by the drinking of nectar.

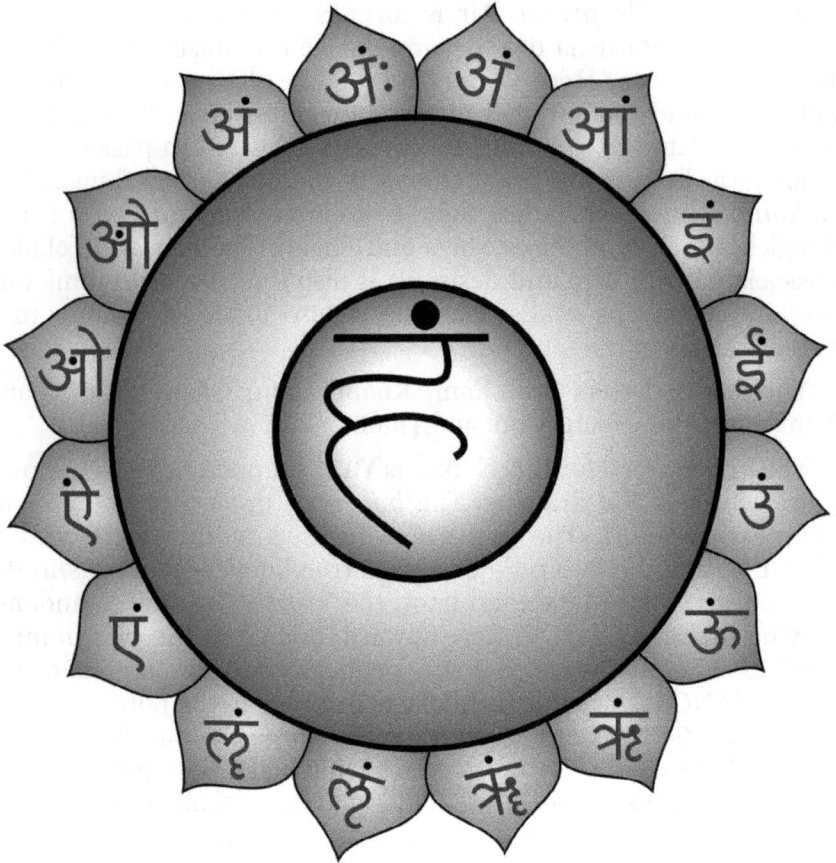

Vishuddha Chakra

## Vishuddha Chakra: Spirit; *akasha*

In Sanskrit the word *shuddha* or *shuddhi* means 'pure'. Pure in this sense is beyond good and evil, right and wrong, purity and impurity. Vishuddha means 'absolutely pure'—for it is free of all such dualistic determinations. The *vishuddha* chakra is associated with the sense of hearing, as well as the action of speaking, and is located in the throat and ear region in the subtle anatomy. The *tattva* of *spirit* or *akasha* is an indigo or violet circle. The *akasha* is within the pure essence (*tanmatra*) of sound (*nada*). At the *vishuddha* chakra, the *sadhaka* gets the vision of *akasha*, which pervades all of space. Akasha is generated by the *tanmatra* of sound.

In the *vishuddha* chakra all the elements of the lower chakras are refined to their purest essence and entirely dissolved in *akasha*. The influence of the five elements ceases after the fifth chakra and the *sadhaka* becomes a *tattvatita*, one who has gone beyond the realm of the elements.

The sixteen letters are: Am, Ām, Im, Îm, Um, Ûm, Ṛm, Ṛm, Lrim, Lrīm, Em, Aim, Om, and Aum, plus the two breathings: Am and Ah.[55]

The *bija mantra* for this chakra is HAM sounded as HANG, seated upon a white elephant. The 'H' sound in the *bija mantra* HANG is produced at the back of the throat. The *mantra* is focused in the throat chakra. When this sound is produced effectively, it awakens the higher intellect (*boddhi*), bringing sweet and melodious qualities to the voice. The deity is Panchavaktra Shiva, who appears with five heads and four arms, and the Shakti is Shakini in the form of light (Jyoti-svarupa). The Lord is also named Sadādhiva, who appears as an androgyne or with a body half white and half gold.

---

[55] The seventh and eighth letters are different: ri and rī, ऋं and ॠं.

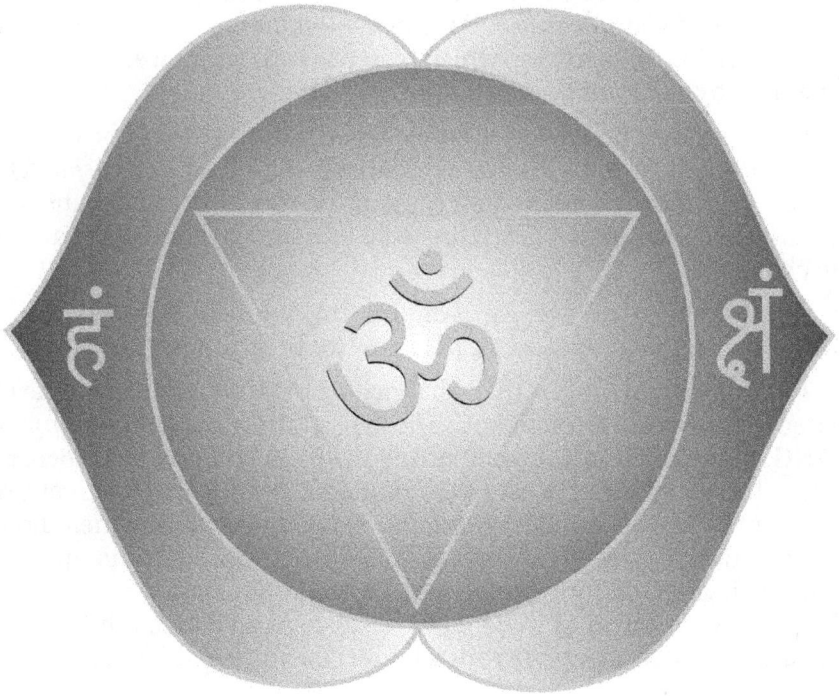

Ajna Chakra

## Ajna Chakra: Mahatattva

Ajna means 'command' or 'summoning' (of the guru). Those who master this chakra of the 'third eye' above the brows eradicate all of their *karmas* and impurities and prepare to enter the seventh door, beyond the *ajna* chakra. The symbol for this chakra is a circle with two petals on either side. AUM is sometimes placed within a triangle.

The yogin who has reached this level of awareness constantly radiates the vibration AUM. The influence of such persons enables all those who come into their presence to become calm and sensitive to the refined spiritual influence of AUM. In *ajna* are the subtle *tattvas* of Mind and Prakriti. All aspects of mind are here, up to and including *boddhi*.

The five great elements (*mahabhutas*)—earth, water, air, fire and *ether* are determinations of *mahatattva*, the supreme or great element in which all other elements are present in their pure essence. Here, Atma shines lustrous as a flame. The yogin draws all his *prana* here at the time of death and enters the primordial state.

The two letters on the petals are Ham (Shiva) and Kṣam (Shakti), left and right. The *bija mantra* for this chakra is AUM. The *bija mantra* AUM is created from three sounds, A, U, and M. The *mantra* AUM is focused in the third eye chakra. The Pravana, AUM, is the source of all sounds and is connected with *anahatha nada*, the primal cosmic vibration. It is thus of the essence of unity and is a combination of Sun (A), Moon (U), and Fire (M).

The third eye plays an important role in the piercing of the third knot, Rudra Granthi. When Rudra Granthi is pierced, individuality is transcended and pure consciousness is experienced in the *sahasrara* chakra. The deities of *ajna* are Shiva and Shakti, united in one form. Paramashiva is also named Hamsa-rupa. The Shakti is also Siddha Kali or the white Hākini-Shakti, 'drunk on ambrosia'—that is, ecstatic or in bliss.

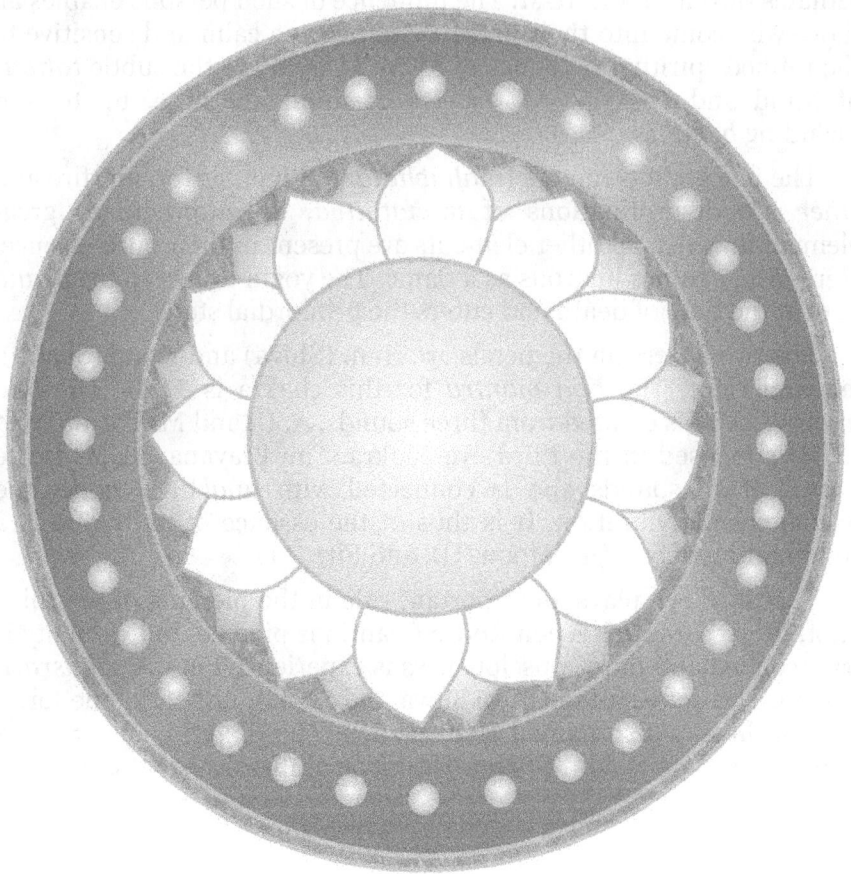

Sahasrara Chakra

## Sahasrara Chakra: Infinite

In Sanskrit the word *sahasrara* means 'thousand', so the *sahasrara* chakra is the Lotus of the Thousand Petals and is said to be located four finger-breadths above the crown of the head. One thousand is a symbolic number and in reality *sahasrara* is numberless, eternal and not limited by space. When the Kundalini is raised up to the *sahasrara* chakra, the illusion of the individual self is dissolved. According to the *shrutis*, the *sahasrara* chakra is the seat of the self-luminous Self, the essence of Pure Being.

Sahasrara is above all *tattvas* and is the light of all lights, without which there would be no light to illumine the universe. Of these countless rays, 360 illumine the world in the form of Fire, Sun and Moon. Agni (Fire) has 118 rays, Sun 106 and Moon 136. These together compose Kala, time, and all measurements, by command of the Lord of the Universe.

All sounds from AH to KSHA are associated with this chakra, including all the vowels and consonants of the Sanskrit alphabet. According to some, AUM can be used for this chakra as it contains all the sounds of the Sanskrit alphabet. According to others, AH can be used as a mantra. Properly speaking, there is nothing to be sounded, whether internally or externally, with the *sahasrara* chakra. One might say that AUM is 'heard', but not as a sound as such. This chakra concerns the Supreme Identity and so it is more about the realisation of the infinite. In the *sahasrara*, Shiva and Shakti are united perfectly.

This ends the Book of Fifty Gates or Letters.[56]

---

[56] It is interesting that in the Qabalah there are also Fifty Gates attributed to the Shekinah, who is the direct equivalent of Kundalini Shakti.

# The Siddhis or Magical Powers

Yoga is designed to transform all those elements in the human being that pose an obstacle to the goal of union with the Universal. It serves to prepare for that union by the use of rhythms, for example the control of breath and the utterance of sonic mantras or sacred syllables. These are preliminary means. Of all such means, theoretical knowledge—which includes not only that of yoga but also the six *vedangas* or traditional sciences—is indispensible. While theoretical knowledge alone is not sufficient in itself it acts as a very necessary support to the goal of Self-Realisation. The path is one of contemplation, which involves assimilation of knowledge through reflective thought, and meditation, when that is understood in the technical sense of *dharana* 'concentration' and *dhyana* 'knowledge'. It is concentration that matters the most for that alone leads to true meditation. This is not in any way comparable with ordinary thought or mere absence of thought; it is itself the fruit of knowledge that is the goal, and that can alone lead to metaphysical realisation. Such realisation is not always complete, which is to say the final supreme state may not have been attained, even if higher states are reached. It can be said then there are lesser degrees of realisation, which all the observances of Ashtanga Yoga are there to support.

The yogin is in reality one who has realised the perfect and final union, which means they have realised the ultimate of all that is possible for the human being. So when this term *yogin* is used as descriptive of mere practitioners it suffers some degradation. The lesser states belong to the yogin too, but they are never considered to be of much importance compared to the totality of existence. The same applies to the Supernormal Powers, otherwise called *siddhis* or 'magical powers' in the Western Tradition. These powers are never pursued for their own sake—or at least, the *Yoga-Sutras* include severe warnings against this. They must be realised as ultimately of an illusionary nature. For that reason the true yogin will generally only use such powers in rare and exceptional circumstances. The warnings exist because the powers can become serious obstacles to further progress. Those who would show off or exhibit peculiar or extraordinary faculties, which includes those in the domain of the supernatural, are never true yogins. The real yogin is one that has, through metaphysical realisation, become entirely and permanently free from all illusory limitations upon the Self and has therefore entered the supra-individual order.

The *siddhis* should therefore never be sought after as an end in itself but there is a need to be aware of them, as they tend to manifest as Kundalini Shakti ascends the lotuses. The following descriptions are as given in the *Shiva Samhita*, with some adaptation and further warnings added.

*Muladhara*: The *darduri siddhi* is the power to leap like a frog and levitate or rise into the air. The master of the chakra becomes free from disease and acquires longevity. He is able to clearly see the past, present and future. He becomes master of all esoteric sciences. He can attain *mantra siddhi* by mere repetition. He is freed from all sins (*karmas*) and attains whatever the mind desires through control of the mind. One should beware that owing to the nature of the root chakra, powerful attachments to objects can arise and that the root of the other lotuses is also the primary root of fear.

*Svadisthana*: Knowledge of all the sciences. Freedom from disease and the ability to go anywhere in the universe at will and without fear. The power to become very great or small also obtains here. One should beware that this chakra can release powerful fears, sense of guilt, lust, jealousy, sin and so forth, in the one that is by no means a master of his self.

*Manipura*: Attainment of all desires. The power to convert base metals to gold, clairvoyance, to find cures for diseases, and to see hidden treasure. One should beware that this chakra, owing to its being linked to the fire element, arouses in the unprepared person an uncontrollable urge to action (or restlessness), and also strong dislikes, plus afflictions such as anger and hatred.

*Anahatha*: Clairvoyance and power of seeing into the past, the present and future. The yogin can walk on air (*khechari siddhi*) and travel anywhere in the universe (*bhuchari siddhi*). The power of knowing other yogins can arise, by which is really meant the power by which gurus can recognise their kin. One should beware that the spiritual love associated with this chakra can also manifest in its inferior forms, for example uncontrollable attachment arising from desire for some person or thing.

*Vishuddha*: Knowledge of the secrets of the Vedas—or of any sacred texts. Strength to overcome weakness, whether in the body or mind. One should beware that while this chakra is at a relatively exalted level, corresponding to the *akasha*, its inferior manifestations may include being 'spaced out'—by which is meant loss of the sense of orientation or otherwise dissociation of mind, owing to the spatial limits being transcended.

*Ajna*: One attains all the fruits of meditation on the chakras below. One who has the knowledge and mastery of this chakra can call on its power at any time, whether standing, walking, wide awake or sleeping, and may become free of sin.

*Sahasrara*: One knows oneself as a god or has the realisation of the Lord of the Universe, or beyond that to the Supreme Identity.

## Selected Works of Oliver St. John

*Hermetic Astrology* (2015)

*Magical Theurgy* (2015)

*The Enterer of the Threshold* (2016)

*Liber 373 Astrum Draconis* (2017)

*Hermetic Qabalah Foundation—Complete Course* (2018)

*Babalon Unveiled! Thelemic Monographs* (2019)

*Ritual Magick—Initiation of the Star and Snake* (2019)

*Nu Hermetica—Initiation and Metaphysical Reality* (2021)

*The Way of Knowledge in the Reign of Antichrist* (2022)

*Thirty-two paths of Wisdom* (2023)

*Thunder Perfect Gnosis—Intellectual Flower of Mind* (2023)

*The Law of Thelema—Hidden Alchemy* (2024)

*Metamorphosis—Hermetic Science and Yoga Power* (2024)

*Dreaming Thelema and Magical Art* (2024)

*Egyptian Tarot and Guide Book* (2025)


The dates given are of first publication. All works published prior to 2021 have since been extensively revised and new editions produced.


Contact the O∴A∴

Universal Gnostic Collegium: Contact details and information is posted on our website at www.ordoastri.org

www.ingramcontent.com/pod-product-compliance
Lightning Source LLC
Chambersburg PA
CBHW060411090426
42734CB00011B/2283